Praise For

BADASS GRIEF

"Anyone who has experienced loss, a significant life event, or a turning point should read *Badass Grief*. It's poignantly written yet also exemplifies how one can draw strength and overcome the most grievous circumstances by facing fear head-on. Jennifer Hassel has delivered a truly inspiring book that will serve as a useful resource for anyone who wants to know how to navigate in uncharted waters."

—Sandra L. Stosz, Vice Admiral, US Coast Guard (Ret.), and Author of *Breaking Ice & Breaking Glass: Leading in Uncharted Waters*

"*Badass Grief* is a heartfelt story of rising past adversity with purposeful courage in the midst of unspeakable and unexpected loss. Hassel's authentic journey demonstrates the complicated link between mourning and moving forward. It invigorates and inspires. A wonderful read!"

—Joanne P. McCallie, Former Duke University Women's Basketball Team Head Coach, and Author of *Secret Warrior: A Coach and Fighter, On and Off the Court*

"Wherever you are on your journey, Jennifer Hassel is here to help you find the courage and strength you need to take your next step."

—Holley Gerth, *Wall Street Journal* Best-Selling Author, Creator of the Heal After You're Hurt course

"*Badass Grief* is a riveting account of Jennifer Hassel's climb—sometimes quite literally—from the heartbreak of early widowhood to a purposeful 'second act.' Readers will find inspiration on every courageously written page."

—Judy Gruen, Author of *Bylines and Blessings: Overcoming Obstacles, Striving for Excellence, and Redefining Success*

"*Badass Grief* will be a gift to anyone who has experienced the loss of a spouse and is wondering how they will go on. With heart and humor, Jennifer Hassel recounts how she revived her own life through a series of incredible challenges designed to honor her husband's philosophy to 'live fully.' While few widows might choose to bear their grief through completing feats like a 100-mile bike race or heli-skiing, everyone will be inspired by her adventures. Jennifer's writing is as strong as her resolve to honor her husband's life, and you will be captivated both by her words and her spirit."

—Kathy Izard, Author of *The Hundred Story Home*, *The Last Ordinary Hour*, and *Trust the Whisper*

"*Badass Grief* embeds in your heart from the start, steadily bringing tears and laughter, as we join Jennifer Hassel on an extraordinary ride from devastating loss to reinvention and emotional transformation. Setting out to honor the spirit and drive of her late husband, Jennifer challenges herself with headshaking endeavors outside her comfort zone, from helicopter powder skiing, a century bike race, and a tri-fitness competition to volunteering in a homeless shelter and traveling to Peru to devote herself to missionary work. Especially for those who have experienced loss, her courageous journey is chock-full of uncommon hope and inspirational rejuvenation."

> —Nancy Pickard, Author of *Bigger Better Braver: Conquer Your Fears, Embrace Your Courage, and Transform Your Life*

"This inspiring memoir tells the story of challenges faced and obstacles overcome, but it does more than that; the author's story gives us an inside view of her varied experiences—from working with the homeless to tackling a CMH heli-skiing adventure. Jennifer shares with us both the painful and laugh-out-loud funny moments we can encounter in loss. Honest and vulnerable, this is a book worth reading."

> —Rob Rohn, President and COO of CMH Heli-Skiing & Summer Adventures

"*Badass Grief* is a powerful testament to resilience, self-agency, and love. In the beginning, Jennifer Hassel survives the death of her young husband through sheer will and commitment to the daily chores of life, including raising three teenagers on her own. Her ultimate survival and rebirth, however, lead her to embrace both physical and emotional challenges willingly. At first she confronts these challenges in memory of her husband and their life together. Ultimately, she realizes that taking on these adventures recreate a brave individual content in herself. This is a courageous and moving book."

> —R. Barbara Gitenstein, President Emerita, the College of New Jersey, Author of *Experience Is the Angled Road: Memoir of an Academic*

"An uplifting tribute to a beloved young doctor lost to cancer. Guided by courage and perseverance, Jennifer Hassel finds a unique way to ensure that her husband's memory will not be forgotten. A terrific, inspiring story!"

> —David M. Zacks, Esq., Past National Chair of the American Cancer Society

Badass Grief:
Changing Gears, Moving Forward

By Jennifer E. Hassel

© Copyright 2024 Jennifer E. Hassel

ISBN 979-8-88824-265-0

All rights reserved. No part of this publication may be reproduced, stored in a retrieval system, or transmitted in any form or by any means—electronic, mechanical, photocopy, recording, or any other—except for brief quotations in printed reviews, without the prior written permission of the author.

Published by

3705 Shore Drive
Virginia Beach, VA 23455
800-435-4811
www.koehlerbooks.com

BADASS GRIEF

CHANGING GEARS, MOVING FORWARD

JENNIFER E. HASSEL

VIRGINIA BEACH
CAPE CHARLES

For Mark, who taught me how to face my fears.

TABLE OF CONTENTS

AUTHOR'S NOTE: 1

CHAPTER 1: 3
What am I doing, and how did life lead me here?

CHAPTER 2: 20
Can I find a suitable way to honor Mark's legacy?

CHAPTER 3: 28
Can I do a good enough job as a single mom while struggling with my own grief?

CHAPTER 4: 37
Do I have the courage to embrace what is strong and beautiful within me?

CHAPTER 5: 57
Can I take my own physical pain and use it in honor of Mark and in recognition of what he endured?

CHAPTER 6: 72
Can I gain perspective on my grief through hearing and seeing firsthand the problems of those who have no home?

CHAPTER 7: 80
Can I find a framework for my life by going back to school and becoming a nurse?

CHAPTER 8: **96**
  Can I make a difference, and if so, how?

CHAPTER 9: **112**
  Do I want to be *fully alive* despite ongoing grief?

PHOTOS **119**

CHAPTER 10: **125**
  Can I find my voice to tell my story?

CHAPTER 11: **135**
  Is another man necessary to fill the hole left by my husband's death?

CHAPTER 12: **152**
  Can I accept my mental and physical limitations with humility rather than as humiliation?

CHAPTER 13: **166**
  Can I truly love again?

EPILOGUE: **177**
  Can I inspire others with my story?

ACKNOWLEDGMENTS **180**

AUTHOR'S NOTE

Anyone who sets out to write about what she experienced is faced with memory limitations. I am no different. I've tried to be a credible narrator but realize that others who participated in these events may remember things differently. What I've written tells the story from my perspective and is based on what I wrote in my journal or what I recall. May the reader grant grace to me and the other humans I encountered. Our priorities and emotions, then and now, obviously filtered the process of determining what we saw and, as a result, what we concluded. For the record, the chronology of events is faithful to what happened, although one challenge I repeated twice was condensed to appear as a single episode.

In writing this story, I'm making the following argument. Remembering and taking action to honor the spirit of someone you love carries his or her memory forward while helping you reclaim life and become a better version of yourself. Let me explain. Among his many qualities, my husband Mark liked to live with gusto. In deciding to remember him through concrete action, I chose to look for ways to say yes to experiences that stretched me. This book is about a few of the exploits I completed in Mark's memory and the life lessons I learned through doing them. I recognize that two of these adventures required the type of resources not many people have. That may be off-putting to some readers. Yet the concept I'm attempting to share is not one that requires money. Living out a legacy is something that almost anyone can do. Basically, you think of any admirable quality of your loved one and then decide on a way to show that quality in your own life. For example, anyone can choose to adopt traits like thoughtfulness, curiosity, compassion, humor, or kindness in their loved one's memory. In whatever way seems fitting under the circumstances, I hope others will adopt the idea of a legacy challenge to remember and live out the spirit of their own loved one.

CHAPTER 1

What am I doing, and how did life lead me here?

THE MOUNTAINS ARE CALLING

Outfitted with an avalanche transceiver, emergency gear, and a two-way radio, I pushed my shoulder into the thick wooden door to step into an overcast January morning. Earlier that week, Arctic winds spilled through gaps in the Northern Canadian Rockies, resulting in temperatures below zero degrees Fahrenheit at Bugaboo Lodge, several hours west of Banff. I leaned into the cold, digging the heels of my ski boots into the narrow, snow-shoveled path to keep from slipping. The helipad was a short walk away. When I arrived, two guides were already piling skis in parallel heaps. The Bell 212 transport helicopter, which would serve as our personal ski lift, would appear soon.

Joining a group of nine other vacationers, I made small talk, trying to tamp down my rising fear. When I'd signed up to go on a heli-skiing trip, the representative assured me it was the beginner group, I'd be in good hands, and this adventure was within my abilities as an intermediate skier. I wanted to believe her.

Judging from the noisy laughter and fake punches, the others seemed in high spirits. And why not? Thoughts of descending through the pristine forests of British Columbia on virgin powder was a skier's dream. They looked forward to being dropped off in waist-deep powder at the top of a 10,000-foot granite plateau in the middle of untouched wilderness. An international camaraderie had already begun to form among those who had arrived from Korea, Belgium, Germany, and the United States the previous day, everyone drawn like iron to magnets for this singular experience. I wanted to be part of it all but felt doubt constrict my chest, as if tiny veins of ice were growing from my spine and encircling my ribs. Just a few feet away from a group of people who seemed so happy, I felt momentarily alone.

To distract myself, I stared at the peaks of the Bugaboo Range, which huddled around us on three sides. The line showing where the snow-jacketed mountains ended and the wispy white sky began was difficult to discern. Both were the color of a dove's wings.

"Your first time in Canada, eh?"

I turned my head toward the skier who spoke to me, his face hidden beneath a helmet, sunglasses, and neck gaiter. I heard the smile in his greeting and responded with one of my own. We introduced ourselves. He had flown in from South Korea with his wife, her sister, and a few friends. More introductions.

Meanwhile, two other European skiers continued to poke fun at the Canadian colloquialism, their French accents adding to the joke as mock questions shot back and forth, each ending with "eh?" A few snowballs were tossed playfully. The more earnest began doing warm-up stretches. Taking it all in, I remembered why I was there, grinning as I thought about my friends back home teasing me that I was a "Bond girl" for going on this trip. I gave myself a brief pep talk. *You got this. It's going to be great.*

We heard the helicopter before we could see it, the distinct rotor sound causing everyone's eyes to turn. The throbbing buzz grew louder. In short order, one of the guides shouted, "Heli huddle!" and pointed to where our group was to squat down, close together, knees in the snow. We complied as instructed, then immediately braced ourselves against the swirl of backwashed air as the copter's skids touched down precisely six feet away.

Once the pilot gave a thumbs-up, the closest skier partially stood and reached to pull down on the handle. The metal door slid back with a bang, and one by one, we hurried to cram into the cabin and slide across the webbed benches that faced each other. Since there was just two feet of space in the middle, we quickly figured out how to angle our knees so we could all fit. Meanwhile, the guides loaded our ski equipment into a caged basket attached to the landing skid on the opposite side. Two minutes later, strapped in and shoulder to shoulder with the others, I felt the sensation of the lift, the steep bank as the pilot turned up the valley, and the ascension over the mountains. The exhilaration of this long-awaited day was finally settling in. A fellow skier handed me his cell phone. "Take our picture!" he shouted, trying to be heard. He leaned toward his buddy and posed with two thumbs up.

I fumbled with my ski gloves but took a few shots before returning the phone. Excitement and trepidation merged as I looked out the window. Cliffs, snow-crusted trees, and steep ravines rushed past. In a few minutes, the helicopter would touch down on a mountaintop almost two miles above sea level, just long enough for us to jump out. Then, the true adventure would begin.

A BADASS WOLVERINE

After dumping its human cargo, the pilot waited for our guide to give the hand signal indicating he was clear to take off. I watched the belly of the helicopter recede and heard the sound of the retreating rotor blades grow fainter until, eventually, all was silent. Except for each other, we were alone, miles from the lodge or any other hint of civilization. At this point, skiing down was my only option, but what I saw was breathtaking for the wrong reasons.

Two years had passed since I'd last been on skis, so I wanted this first run to be easy. In my mind, I'd envisioned zigzagging across wide-open slopes pillowed with deep, fluffy expanses of snow while I got reacclimated to skiing and learned to make turns through powder, which feels quite different from navigating groomers in Colorado. In actuality, our first run involved a steep drop-off into groves thick with spruce and hemlock, their branches stretched out treacherously. Looking down the mountain, I had several concerns—the powder was thigh-high, it was difficult to maintain my balance on the fat skis attached to my boots, I had arthritic knees, *and* we were going to be in trees. Trees!

One of the guides pointed the way with his ski pole and started down, creating a path for the first skiers to follow. Despite my apprehension, I pushed off and began a barely controlled descent.

Though you often hear how certain things are "like riding a bicycle," meaning that you don't forget how to do them, that isn't exactly true. After just three awkward turns, I had my first fall. How embarrassing. I struggled back up, cleaned the snow from my goggles, and immediately took off again, not wanting to display my fear. Not long thereafter, I attempted to avoid a scraggly pine barely three feet tall, made the mistake of looking at it, and, as a result, crashed straight into the trunk. I tripped and did a faceplant in deep snow, unable to move because my legs were buried behind me at a steep angle. Mercifully, the rest of the group was ahead, so they missed my clumsy cartwheel. A guide immediately appeared at my side, dug out both my skis, and helped me clip back into them.

"I'm going to make you earn your keep today," I said, trying to cover my humiliation at having fallen twice in the first few minutes.

He made light of my incompetence. "Actually, I'm lucky. How many guys get paid to pick up women?"

Despite his smile, I couldn't help but observe that no one in the group seemed to be having this much trouble. Another guide noticed it, too. She skied over to where we stood and introduced herself.

"I'm Kathy. Let me help you."

Seeing that I was in capable hands, the first guide left to catch up with everyone else. Kathy and I were alone.

"The main issue is that your fear is causing you to lean back," she said, summarizing the stance many of us take when we're afraid of something. "Let's just take a moment."

The tone of her voice was kind, and I felt relieved. Kathy's willingness to give me time to collect myself allowed me to stop hurrying. I'd felt pressure to keep up with the group, not wanting to be the slowest, the one everyone else had to wait for. This inner tension, along with the fear of careening out of control into a tree, obviously didn't help my skiing. Kathy's presence made it okay to be still. I sucked in a lungful of frigid air and blew it out hard. My chest was heaving from adjusting to the altitude and working to get back up after my latest fall. Kathy studied me.

"Breathe like this," she said evenly. As she spoke, Kathy demonstrated. "First, take a deep breath through your nostrils, hold it just a moment, then exhale slowly through your mouth." I did so.

"Again," she instructed.

Kathy stood next to me, and together, we breathed in solidarity. This allowed my tangled mind to detach from the shame engendered by my string of falls and the resulting vulnerability of feeling somehow less than everyone else in the group. Kathy was the ski whisperer, and I was the frightened acolyte. Her very presence was calming.

I focused intently, and we took another five slow, deep breaths. This deliberate breathing was effective at relaxing the knots of my fisted self. Kathy didn't rush me. Once I was more composed, she pointed out that we all get afraid sometimes.

"I'm going to share a secret with you," she said, leaning

toward me. "When I get scared, I force myself to stand up straight. I take a deep breath and imagine a fierce spirit animal giving me courage. I usually think of a wolverine. I tell myself, 'I am a *badass wolverine*!'"

She looked into my eyes. "Now it's your turn. Give it a try," she coaxed. "Say it out loud and with conviction!"

My voice wavered as I repeated her mantra in a barely audible voice. "I . . . am a . . . badass . . . wolverine." Kathy ignored my lack of buy-in.

"After that, I say, 'Thank you, fear—I got this!'" She looked at me again and said, "Now your turn."

I drew back a bit, somewhat surprised. Apparently, I hadn't heard her correctly, but what *I thought* I'd heard actually motivated me. Emboldened by what I took as permission to get in fear's face, I lifted my chin and yelled skyward with full conviction, "FUCK YOU, FEAR! I got this!"

Having convinced myself of my resolve, I pushed off with solid determination, found I could make the necessary turns despite the steep pitch and numerous trees, and caught the group further down the slope, feeling strong and exhilarated.

During our five days of heli-skiing, there would be many opportunities to practice Kathy's mind tool and my take on it. I was a sixty-two-year-old suburban woman, an average skier at best, who didn't like being cold and had serious reservations about all the ways this trip could go south: hitting a tree, getting caught in an avalanche, going over an unmarked cliff, or falling into a tree well. There was a genuine risk of serious bodily injury—or worse—yet here I was. What could have led me to push the limits of my capabilities by choosing to go on a heli-skiing adventure? How did the decision to pursue life with gusto crawl out from beneath the depression and anguish that formed after death claimed one of my own way too soon? Before sharing, however, I'd like to offer some background.

AN EARLY DECISION

When I was in sixth grade, my dad, a sailboat broker, made an offhand remark that I should be a lawyer when I grew up. I had no idea what a lawyer did, but then and there, I decided to become one. Such is the mystical power of parental belief in one's capabilities. If he thought it was possible, so did I. Even without knowing what becoming a lawyer meant, I sensed it was a worthy aspiration. My goal was set.

A fresh wind filled my small sail, and I adjusted course accordingly. Over the next seven years, I mentally revisited my career choice but never found any other that seemed better. I went to college thinking that I would eventually go to law school. Having a set bearing gave me an anchor to hold onto while all around me, my peers seemed adrift, fretfully trying to figure out what to do with their lives. Not me. I already knew.

The simple strategy of setting a focal point and then moving toward it has repeatedly helped me tame my anxiety whenever I face confusing, alarming, or overwhelming circumstances.

Step by step, I proceeded with my career plan until I had graduated with honors from law school, took and passed the Pennsylvania bar exam, and landed my first job, a prestigious clerkship with a federal judge in the eastern district of Pennsylvania. Working in the United States courthouse, an impressive building on Independence Mall overlooking the Liberty Bell, was exciting for a new lawyer. I had a front-row seat to the judge's entire docket, including two mob-related racketeering trials involving characters with nicknames that gave indications of sociopathic tendencies.

While my legal career was evolving, so was my personal life. One of my hobbies was participating in endurance-based sports. During my judicial clerkship, I started training for a competition with the newly formed Philadelphia Triathlon Club. A weekend group ride into the suburbs proved to be life-changing when my bike chain broke. A guy I didn't know stopped to help me. His name was Mark. After using two rocks to tentatively hammer the chain back together, he rode beside me the whole way back to the city. On the bigger hills, he put his hand on the small of my back and pushed me upward to reduce stress on the compromised chain.

He was smart, funny, and unassuming, a second-year medical student whose confident smile and broad shoulders convinced me to ignore his nerdy glasses and badly cut hair. I liked him immediately, and apparently, the feeling was mutual. We quickly became inseparable. Three years later, we married.

The week following our wedding, we left Philadelphia because Mark earned a coveted residency in dermatology at the Medical College of Georgia. At the time, there were about 200 first-year residency spots for dermatology in the United States. We loaded our belongings into Mark's 1979 VW Rabbit and moved to Augusta. After passing the Georgia bar exam, I worked at a small law firm near the hospital where Mark learned the intricacies of skin diseases and their treatment.

It took three years for Mark to complete his residency. He was then selected for a prestigious two-year fellowship in dermatologic surgery at NYU Medical Center in Manhattan. We relocated to New York, and I found a job as an associate with a Wall Street law firm. Our first child, Erin, was born during our last year in the city that never sleeps. Once Mark's training was finally complete, we decided to move to Lancaster, Pennsylvania, to raise our family. Mark had grown up there, and I fell in love with the beautiful farmlands and vibrant small-town community.

THE GOOD DOCTOR

Mark opened a solo practice in dermatologic surgery, and I joined a well-regarded local law firm. While it sounds smooth and neat to say that he did this and I did that, it was anything but. Setting up a solo medical practice from scratch is an epic undertaking that few attempted thirty years ago and probably none do now. There is a simple reason. Medical practice is unusual because it has Byzantine rules that must be mastered to get paid. This is a formidable challenge but only the first of many. Front office and medical staff must be hired and trained, and expensive and specialized equipment must be selected and installed. Add to that choosing and learning a computer system, marketing the practice, designing the office, overseeing the construction, and meeting with banks to finance the undertaking. These are a few of the challenges that were on Mark's to-do list before he could open his doors to actually practice medicine. Only someone with bare-balls gutsiness can dare think of being up to the task. Mark was that kind of someone. He accomplished the near impossible, and the DermaSurgery Center opened for business in the summer of 1991.

Twelve years passed. Two more children were born, Emily and Carson. I decided to give up my legal career to stay home full time. I was in the enviable position of not having to work. Mark's medical practice flourished to the point that there was often a three- to six-month wait to get an appointment. His professional specialty was dermatologic surgery, but Mark was also gifted in connecting with people of all ages. While some physicians enter a room with a "Here I am" posture, Mark invariably put others at ease with his "Ah, there you are" warmth.

He used simple language to explain complex medical ideas and had funny stories to share with his patients as he performed uncomfortable procedures. His uncanny ability to mimic animal sounds was a particular favorite with the pediatric set. One frightened ten-year-old needed a wart removed from her hand. Mark told her that yes, it would sting, but the pain would be over by the time she counted to five, and afterward, he would personally imitate any animal she requested.

"Can you do an elephant?"

"An elephant? Of course, I can."

This happened to be one of Mark's most impressive sound reproductions. Our children and their friends requested "the elephant" regularly. It was that good. The small patient bravely held still, and then she and her mother laughed as Dr. Mark put down his instruments and trumpeted like a bull elephant, using his right arm to indicate a lifted trunk.

Going about daily life in a small town, I frequently heard compliments toward Dr. Mark. At my hair salon, one of the stylists shared how grateful she was for my husband. Her hands had been peeling, red, and sore, a reaction to the chemicals in hair products. This dermatitis was painful and threatened her ability to make a living for her family. During her appointment, Mark gently took her face into his own hands, looked into her eyes, and said, "I am so sorry this happened to you. I'm going to do everything I can to help you."

Another time, I learned how Mark was to perform an extensive reconstructive surgery on a toddler with a facial deformity. The morning of the procedure, he met the family in the preoperative holding area. Rather than have the child strapped to a gurney to be wheeled into the operating room, Mark talked to the boy for a time, made him laugh, and then lifted and carried him down the hall to surgery while making jet noises. I imagined the surprised nurse trotting behind them, straining to keep up with Mark's long stride. Later, the parents told Mark how this interaction reassured them that their son would be treated not just well but lovingly.

Often, when I think back to those days, I see our three children and their friends hanging off Mark or circling him, calling his name and vying for his attention. He was the dad in the pool tossing the ball or the kids themselves while the rest of us sat in the shade with our cold drinks. When we went on a family hike, he led our brood into the creek to look for crayfish and salamanders, unconcerned about whether he got soaked or muddy. He made up games to play with our kids after dinner involving running and dodging to avoid being hit with a squishy ball. Despite needing to body-swerve furniture, lamps, and each other during indoor ball tag, only a few nonessential objects and one of Mark's toes broke in the process.

His distinctive laughter was inevitable whenever he was around children—a long, slightly wheezy inhale followed by a silent pause at the apex, then a donkey-like decrescendo, deep and sonorous. No one could imitate it, though we had fun trying. The effort always brought another round of laughter.

In addition to his practice, Mark was an adjunct professor of dermatology. One morning, our fourth-grade daughter, Emily, noticed that her dad was dressed in a suit and tie rather than his typical surgical scrubs.

"Why are you all dressed up, Daddy?"

"I'm going to Hershey to teach other doctors today."

"You're teaching other doctors? Wow, Daddy, you're even smarter than I thought!"

Emily wasn't the only one who thought this. Mark himself would deny being intellectually gifted. "I just work hard," he would say, but other people would comment that Mark was among the smartest people they'd ever met.

My husband was someone who exemplified the statement, "Live fully!" He would embrace every opportunity to explore, travel, taste exotic foods, or try unfamiliar things. I admired his courage and occasionally attempted to keep up, although I could never do anything at his level. He was thrilled by the challenge of skiing the rock-lined chutes in Deer Valley's Empire Canyon and the legendary Corbet's Couloir in Jackson Hole. He crawled through the tight-fitting, claustrophobia-inducing limestone caves of West Virginia armed with a headlamp and a smile. He was a certified scuba diver who swam two miles before work most mornings. Once, he jumped off a cliff in tandem with an instructor to hang glide. I wanted to join him, but my fear of heights held me back. Instead, I watched my hero soaring overhead and took countless pictures.

I liked being active alongside Mark. Our free time was often spent cycling, hiking, skiing, or distance swimming. Actually, it was more like we would start these things together. He was a fit and able-bodied man born with an easy athletic grace. Unless he consciously slowed down to my level, I was forever in his wake, watching his back as he got farther and farther in front of me, no matter the sport.

He carved effortless turns through the tree runs off the Ninety-Nine 90 lift in Park City, then waited for me to attempt to follow by finding an easier route down. When we biked on the quiet roads of Lancaster County, he would sprint ahead, crest the next hill, and then circle back to where I was still plodding along. This often required him to do the same hill twice. If we were swimming at the local YMCA, he would lap me repeatedly. I grew to accept that he would always be in front. There was a comfort in knowing that someone stronger would lead the way.

DON'T IT ALWAYS SEEM TO GO?

Becoming a dermatologic surgeon required ten years of training in addition to four years of college. During that time, we lived modestly, paying off our combined student loans while trying to save for the future. When Mark was finally able to open his practice and begin earning a real living, he was thirty-two. Considering all his gifts, it's no surprise that he was successful. As a result, we eventually built a gorgeous home and took bike trips to Europe. I felt secure in our good fortune, believing we had earned it through diligence and perseverance.

Joni Mitchell's line, "You don't know what you got till it's gone," did not fit us. We both knew that ours was a dream life. We just didn't know that it wouldn't last. In our nineteenth year of marriage, I received three prophetic signs that our world would implode.

First, I had a dream. In it, Mark was at the wheel while we cruised side by side in a small convertible. The top was down, the sky a glorious, sparkling blue. We turned to each other, laughing, ecstatic to have a day to ourselves. Without warning, the nose of the car tipped over an unseen edge, and we began falling into a black valley, out of control. Rigid with terror, I tried to scream as we gained speed. Then, shockingly, I became aware of a shadow even more overwhelming than the heart-stopping descent.

Far across the valley stood a mountain of rock which rose so high that I knew, deeply and inexplicably, it was not of this world. At the sight of it, I forgot about falling and forgot about my husband next to me in the car because my sole focus became that monolith with a top that stretched into and became part of the sky. A primal knowing informed me that what I saw was a reflection of God Himself.

Wait, only dead people face God, right?

I lurched awake, terrified, and reached over to touch my husband's back, the contact reassuring me that we were both alive, safe in our bed.

What would it be like if he wasn't here? I thought.

A few weeks later, my best friend and I were together. A question popped into my mind for no reason at all, so I voiced it.

"What's your worst fear?"

After telling me, she turned the question around. "What's yours?"

"I'm afraid something is going to happen to Mark."

Why had I thought that? What part of my subconscious detected a subterranean shift when there was no surface indication that anything was wrong?

The last sign occurred twenty-four hours before my nightmare stepped over the threshold to become a reality. I was in Philadelphia on a two-night mother-daughter trip with then twelve-year-old Emily. As we shopped in a funky boutique on South Street for a T-shirt souvenir, I felt an aura of foreboding, like an amorphous, pressing dread. I tried to ignore it, thinking it would pass, but as the day wore on, the sensation grew into a full-blown anxious compulsion. *We had to get home.* I had never experienced anything like this, yet I knew there was no choice but to act on it. Trying to keep my voice neutral, even as my uneasiness increased with each passing minute, I turned to Emily.

"Would you mind if we cut this trip a day short? I think we should get back early."

"Sure, Mom."

We took a cab back to the hotel to quickly gather our things. Though it was past 5 p.m., the hotel clerk let us check out without a word. That seemed odd. My sense of panic caused me to press hard on the accelerator the entire ninety-minute ride back to Lancaster. When we walked through the door, Mark was making dinner for our other two children. He was surprised to see us, but nothing seemed amiss. I felt myself calming down in our familiar surroundings, my family together and safe. Why the angst?

The next day, Mark had scheduled three medical appointments for himself. Since I was home and my day was unplanned, I decided to go along with him. His shoulder had been bothering him, so the first appointment was with an orthopedist, one of Mark's colleagues. This man examined the shoulder, did not find anything seriously wrong, and discussed physical therapy as a starting point. From the orthopedist's office, we drove to an outpatient facility where Mark was scheduled for an abdominal ultrasound. He had been experiencing stomach irritation for the past half year, something he attributed to stress. Stress was understandable. Mark was simultaneously running a busy and successful solo dermatology practice while trying to build a new surgery center where he could perform his skin cancer and reconstruction surgeries.

I was sitting with Mark in the darkened room while the ultrasound was performed. Shortly after she started, the tech turned the screen away from Mark's face, but in such a way that neither of us thought it unusual. Afterward, she walked us out and stood watching our backs as we, in blissful ignorance, swung hands while exiting through the sliding electric doors. What did she think as she witnessed our last few minutes as a carefree couple?

After the ultrasound, we headed across town to meet with Mark's primary care doctor, another medical colleague. Mark had been feeling especially run down lately, and we had plans to leave for a hiking trip later that month to celebrate his forty-sixth birthday. I don't know what we discussed in the car, but I remember thinking he probably needed some antibiotics. In the fifteen minutes it took us to drive to the doctor's office, someone from the ultrasound facility had called ahead to convey the findings.

We were herded into a tiny conference room immediately upon our arrival. Moments later, Dr. B walked in with someone else, maybe his nurse. Skipping the preliminaries, he gave us the news. Mark had cancer, and it had spread to his liver. Mark and Dr. B locked eyes for a moment. Immediately, they understood what I did not. We were already beyond hope. Both men began openly weeping.

According to the experts, 2 percent somehow survive a diagnosis of metastatic stomach cancer. Oh, to be in that 2 percent. We tried. So. Very. Hard. Ultimately, we got nineteen more months.

We were alone in our bedroom when I held Mark as he took

his last breath. The transfer from my arms to God's occurred in the quiet hours after midnight as our three children slept upstairs. My brother and his wife dozed in our guest room, where they had camped out to wait for Mark's appointment with death. Days later, our house swelled with family and friends, food and flowers, and so much sadness that it's a wonder the walls didn't crack from the pressing weight of it all. Then, we buried him—my brilliant, wise, strong, athletic, funny, handsome, gifted, and generous husband.

NOW WHAT?

Before he died, Mark once commented how he didn't want people to forget him. The sweet vulnerability of this offhand remark from someone who rarely wanted recognition spread itself over my heart. Without realizing it, Mark had handed me a serious assignment. The little I knew about honoring someone who died involved donating to a cause or putting the person's name on a bench.

The spring after the funeral, I had each of our children write a short, one-page letter to their father. I wrote one, too. A local craftsman made bronze copies of these four epistles and embedded them onto a stone bench I installed by the play area of our yard. Though touching, the exercise was merely a once-and-done snapshot of our family's love. It changed nothing, and I knew it would eventually blend into the landscaping. I wondered if there was something else I could do to maintain Mark's presence in the community and our lives.

Alone at the computer one night, I did a Google search for ideas on how to commemorate someone. A lot of what I found involved giving money or buying something. Some of the suggestions included making a teddy bear or quilt from the deceased's clothing, getting a personalized memorial bird feeder for your yard, planting a tree, sprinkling your loved one's ashes around the tree, donating to a charity, putting your person's name on a plaque, a donor wall, or even your flesh, buying jewelry with their birthstone or thumbprint, or commissioning their portrait.

I did many of these things, but it wasn't enough. I longed for another way to demonstrate a bigger concept—not merely that I missed Mark but that knowing him inspired me to become a better person. People outside our family would never remember Mark or feel the ache of his absence in the same way I did, no matter how often I put his name in front of their eyes. Part of my thinking was also to show our three children that we had a legacy to consider. I wasn't sure what form such a remembrance would take, but I was certain that it had to reflect the dynamic momentum of a man who wasn't afraid to take risks.

Sometimes, you sense that you're looking for something unknown. This notion hangs out on the periphery of your thinking, silently gathering materials and waiting for you to eventually notice how the pieces might fit. As with other sorts of new ideas, the humble beginnings of mine were assembled in a garage.

CHAPTER 2

Can I find a suitable way to honor Mark's legacy?

SQUARE ONE

When your husband dies, he leaves behind tangible evidence of his humanity. His toothbrush sits next to the sink, his wallet and keys are on the nightstand, and his socks are crumbled in a ball where he left them in the corner near the bed. Many people find comfort in keeping things that belonged to their loved ones. For me, looking at his clothes hanging silent and lifeless in our closet or seeing the shoes he would never slip his feet into again were grief triggers. Especially in the first few weeks, I could not protect myself from the painful debridement of making decisions about his stuff, each item a reminder of him, his death, and our loss.

The week after Mark died, I walked to his wood-paneled study and closed the door. Entering that room where he had so often retreated to review medical journals felt like trespassing on sacred ground. Except for that easily avoided part of the house, I purged with intensity over the next few months. I cleared out, gave away, or hid the bulk of his personal effects. I sold his almost-new car, the one he had dubbed "the chemo mobile" because we had used it to make the weekly two-hour trek from our home in Pennsylvania to the Johns Hopkins Cancer Center in Baltimore. The nickname alone was reason enough. Eventually, a lifetime of material accumulation was distilled into what was emotionally manageable. In that emetic season, I could not decide what to do with Mark's Yamaha Vino scooter.

We had purchased it after his diagnosis to give him a way to have a little freedom. An actual motorcycle would have been too heavy, given his declining health. The Vino was a flashy royal-blue beauty. As Mark said, it had enough "snot" to reach 50 mph. We had often explored the rolling farmlands near our home astride its seat. We could act like a normal couple having fun for a few hours. Mark would steer, and I'd sit behind him, arms wrapped around his waist, our helmets clinking together when there was a brief pause as he changed gears. He'd gotten to enjoy it for only six months before becoming too sick to ride.

The scooter remained in the garage, unused, its beautiful paint eventually dulled by a film of dust. A collection of yard toys, garden tools, and discarded cardboard boxes began to form a wall around it. Eventually, the scooter blended into the garage scenery, easily overlooked.

One morning, as I sat with coffee and picked up Mark's Bible, a copy of his funeral program slid onto the table. I flipped it over. On the back side were seven statements that our pastor, a close friend, had been inspired to write about the example of Mark's approach to life.

1. Live fully.
2. Laugh often.
3. Serve others.
4. Be faithful.
5. Suffer courageously.
6. Love nature.
7. Love God.

The first statement stuck in my head like the lyrics to a song. Live fully. One of the reasons I had always admired Mark was his willingness to take risks and try new things, be it hang gliding over the Matterhorn, hiking a 9,000-foot Colorado peak on the spur of the moment, swimming with sharks, or trying vegemite toast.

I thought about how I was trudging through each day, swaddled head to toe in a sadness that prevented me from perceiving much except its confines. *What message am I sending my children?* All they could see was a mom who appeared defeated by circumstance. Their dad was no longer present to teach them how to rebound after tragedy. That was up to me. I needed to demonstrate that their father's death would not keep me (or them) down forever. My focus on rereading the tearful script of what had already happened wasn't helping me cope or setting a good example.

Subconsciously, I reached for the strategy that had served me well. I needed to look toward the horizon for a new focal point. Perhaps action, especially purposeful action, would kickstart me so I could feel something other than hopeless sadness. Since Mark had been someone who lived fully, why couldn't I pick up the baton and carry that ideal forward? Emulating him would honor his memory better than remaining mired in the setting concrete of my grief.

Just the previous night, I'd read a quote from Viktor Frankl's book, *Man's Search for Meaning*, written after the author survived the Holocaust: "Man is capable of changing the world for the better if possible, and of changing himself for the better if necessary."

A change in me was necessary. It was time to set a goal to begin implementing it.

What about that scooter?

I got up from the kitchen table and went to the garage to look. Dusty and half hidden by boxes, the Vino leaned against its kickstand, the front handlebars jauntily angled. Its very presence suggested a different life than the one I was living. In *Roman Holiday*, a classic movie from 1953, Hollywood icon

Audrey Hepburn runs amuck through the streets of Rome on a similar Vespa, a trapped princess escaping from the drudgery of a confined life. Standing in the garage looking at the scooter, I felt a nudge, like a tiny spark of inspiration. Maybe this vehicle was my key to newfound freedom. If I got a motorcycle license, I could get on, ride, and move forward. The mere thought of doing this made me smile.

IT'S GO TIME

The Pennsylvania Department of Transportation offers a free Motorcycle Safety Course consisting of five hours of classroom work and twelve hours of actual riding. Penn DOT supplies the motorcycles. According to its website, all I needed to do was bring my permit and helmet. After scanning the information, I found a nearby course that fit my schedule, studied for and passed the written test to get a motorcycle driving permit, and signed up.

The riding clinic portion of the course was held on an early Saturday in June. Of all places, it met in the parking lot of my husband's high school alma mater. While navigating morning traffic to get there, I could feel my chest thumping, a tight heaviness in my gut. This would be the first time I'd be driving a motorcycle, something women my age typically don't learn to do. I was fifty years old. That sense of being invincible had dried up decades ago.

Though the bikes used by the class weren't exactly huge choppers, they were still heavy and powerful. As with trying anything new, I felt the buzz of anticipation mixed with apprehension. *Can I coordinate throttle, clutch, and foot pedals while also trying to maintain balance and steer?* I didn't even know how to turn the bike on. The instruction book mentioned an engine cut-off switch, adjusting the choke as necessary, holding down the brake, and turning the key. It seemed like a lot to remember, and that was just to get the thing started.

Despite these and other serious reservations, I was determined to give this class my best shot. I took a deep breath and blew it out through pursed lips.

There were six other participants, all men, all twenty or thirty-somethings. I was acutely aware of being the only woman and an older one at that. Even the instructors, called "rider coaches," were men younger than me. Yet, if anyone else saw me as an outlier, it went unacknowledged. I stood up tall and pulled my shoulders back. Regardless of how I felt, the Frye boots I'd borrowed from my daughter helped me think I fit in. Undoubtedly, I was kidding myself.

The coaches were patient and encouraging. "We know some of you have ridden before, but we will assume you know zilch. We'll take it from there."

Hearing this was a relief.

Six hours after throwing my leg over a motorcycle for the first time, I could circle the parking lot with the rest of the class, weave through cones, maintain a safe distance, and even change gears. Practicing these new skills necessitated eliminating everything else from my mind, an unexpected benefit. There's no space left for grief if you are fully absorbed in learning something challenging. Though I struggled a bit with remembering all the steps and my gear shifting needed work, I was sure I'd be able to pass the following week's road test, given the positive trajectory of this first day.

The next Saturday was sunny and sweltering hot, causing shimmery pools to float over the asphalt as we again gathered in the parking lot. Three rider coaches worked with us to learn quick stops, riding over debris, downshifting before curves, and tight turns. We practiced until late in the day. All was going well.

Until it wasn't.

The neurological adaptations that create muscle memory don't happen in an afternoon. Learning to change gears was new to me, so I had to talk myself through the sequential steps deliberately, one after the other: left hand—engage the clutch; right hand—release the throttle; left foot—press the gear lever down (to downshift) or lift it (to upshift). Just as I was beginning to get in the groove, my bike began having mechanical problems, repeatedly revving high regardless of my gear, then stalling out when I attempted to shift.

I tried unsuccessfully to adjust my timing, engaging the clutch faster and waiting a moment before pressing on the gear lever. No luck. Gently easing the clutch in was also unsuccessful. *What am I doing wrong?* I began overthinking the gear shifting, lost my rhythm, and then my confidence tanked.

The rider coaches noticed my struggle and came over to investigate. One, then another, attempted to adjust the bike, yet it still sputtered and stalled. A replacement motorcycle was wheeled out for me, but it had a different feel. The clutch was stiffer, and the bike bucked a few times as I practiced. As with dancing, trying harder usually makes things worse.

The road test was now minutes away, but my self-assurance had evaporated. It seemed I'd reached an inflection point—and not just with the motorcycle class. Perhaps my shortcomings in learning to shift gears hinted at the real problem. In the past, I was used to being in the back, holding onto my husband's waist while he chose the route and steered. *Can I slide into the driver's seat, get out of neutral, and ride forward alone?*

We were given a ten-minute break before the test. I turned away from the group, removed my helmet, found a grassy patch at the parking lot's edge, and slumped down. Not wanting to cry in front of strangers, I dug my fingernails into the palms of my clenched fists.

I don't know what I'm doing.

Caught up in berating myself for failing before I'd even had a chance to see whether I would, I forgot about Mark's inspiration and my desire to set an example for my kids. My head down, I stared at the grass. That's when I saw, right by my foot, a four-leaf clover.

After plucking and examining my prize, I realized I held something truly miraculous—a *five*-leaf clover. A small, fifth leaf lay almost hidden atop the larger fourth leaf. It was like a talisman representing my family: four members visible, a fifth one overlaying my heart. This little green token felt like a cosmic nudge reminding me why I was there.

Mark and I had a thing about four-leaf clovers. Twenty-three years earlier, after our first date in Philadelphia, he and I sat on the grass in Rittenhouse Square, a popular city park.

"Do you think we could find a four-leaf clover?" I asked him. What a ridiculous thing for me to say. A more unlikely place for a four-leaf clover was hardly conceivable. Hundreds of people, vendors, and dogs visited this park daily. The grassy areas were tiny and well-used. Despite these odds, Mark simply glanced down at the patch beside him, immediately picked one up, and handed it to me.

"Here," he'd said.

Throughout our marriage, we found four-leaf clovers at auspicious times. Finding the five-leaf clover was surely a personalized, heaven-sent sign.

I can do this, I told myself.

The tester called us to line up and mount our motorcycles. I was calm as we individually and painstakingly did slow figure eights around orange cones in a taped-off square, then accelerated to third gear before downshifting to a full stop. Afterward, the class stood together in a circle, helmets off, making small talk. A few minutes later, the tester approached our waiting group with his clipboard in front of him. He announced that everyone had passed, then smiled as he added, "Two of you got perfect scores." He turned and held my eyes for a brief moment, pausing for dramatic effect. "Well done, James and Jennifer."

Me!

My smile was immediate, huge, and genuine. In that moment, I felt something awakening, something that cancer had quashed. Happiness. I was truly happy for the first time since Mark's diagnosis two years earlier.

My classmates thumped me on the back, and we all cheered. Then I experienced a surge of affirming energy, as if separate wires had been brought back together and reconnected. Amazement, joy, and then, ultimately, thankfulness passed through me. This emotional kaleidoscope reflected how something beautiful could be created from life's broken bits. I felt a new inner strength along with the accomplishment of doing something I had feared. The success was invigorating.

Driving home after the test, I made a defining decision. Every year moving forward, I would challenge myself to "live fully" by doing one significant, out-of-my-comfort-zone activity in Mark's honor. I would be a living legacy of the adventurous spirit he exemplified. That I could feel happy again by stretching myself toward an ambitious goal renewed my sense of possibility for the future. Maybe it was only a fluke, but perhaps the version of myself I remembered from before Mark's cancer diagnosis could be rekindled.

Things will eventually get better. You will find a way.

CHAPTER 3

Can I do a good enough job as a single mom while struggling with my own grief?

THE SORT OF FATHER HE WAS

When our family was young, I endured the same weekly struggle—how to nourish, clothe, and strap three children into the car to get our family to church by 9:30 a.m. on the so-called day of rest. I was sorely tested to accomplish this objective calmly. Mark frequently intervened when it came to Emily, our particularly distractible middle daughter, who was then five.

One Sunday in March, while I made a last-ditch attempt to throw on some makeup, both daughters decided to get their rabbits out of the hutch to play with them loose in the backyard. Mark was upstairs helping our youngest get dressed. A few minutes later, I was rushing toward the garage.

"Emily! Erin! Time to get in the car."

The girls went to pick up their bunnies, but Beauty, Emily's pet, dashed for freedom. Each time Emily got close, Beauty scooted away. I stood at the back door in high heels, gritting my teeth as I watched Emily try to catch that rabbit. The ground was dotted with patches of snow, and as Emily ran in pursuit, she struggled to keep her footing. She managed the chase just fine. Her clothes did not. Both knees bore grass stains, and her coat and mittens were damp and dirty.

By then, Mark had gotten the other two children in the car.

He returned to the kitchen to assess the situation. We were already running late, and he knew from prior experience and my crossed-arm stance that I was pissy and irritated.

"Go!" he said, gently turning me toward the garage. "I'll help Emily, and we'll drive separately."

They never made it.

I later learned that after a futile five-minute attempt to corner Beauty, Mark had given up and carried a crying Emily to the car. They drove only a mile. From the back seat, Mark heard this imploring small voice choke out her misery.

"Daddy, how would *you feel* if you knew I was outside all alone in the cold? Well, that's how *I feel*." More tears.

He glanced in the rearview mirror, saw her slumped shoulders and downcast eyes, pulled the car over, and turned back toward home.

"Okay, Emily. Let's go get your rabbit."

The crying stopped.

Beauty had taken refuge beneath the backyard playhouse, which rested on cinder blocks. Mark got a broom, laid on the partially frozen, damp ground, and attempted to push the rabbit out the back side so Emily could grab her. Each time he swept the broom toward Beauty, she simply hopped over it. After a few fruitless passes, he paused to reevaluate his strategy. He noticed that he was cold and wet, while an animal with a walnut-sized brain was warm and dry.

He got up and walked over to the garden hose. After turning it on full force, he returned to the playhouse, got down on all fours, and aimed the stream directly at Beauty's rump. It didn't take long for the sopping bunny to retreat from the spray into Emily's waiting arms.

"Thank you, Daddy," Emily said, gratefully looking up at him while nuzzling her drenched pet.

NINE YEARS LATER . . .
THE SORT OF MOTHER I WAS

From the look in her eyes, I believed she thought the wrong parent had died.

"Emily, we argue constantly," I said, exasperated with her again.

"No. We don't," she countered.

Emily was born with her motor revving in third gear. Not wanting to miss a thing, she refused to nap. Ever. If I strapped her in the car seat or a stroller, I quickly learned that her tolerance for being restrained lasted exactly fifteen minutes. After that, she would begin her high-volume wailing while she bucked against the straps and thrashed her tiny arms. She learned to walk at ten months and discovered running shortly after that. When she was a toddler, I searched the bookstore shelves for advice on parenting this small cyclone. I lurched to the cash register, trying to balance *Solving Your Child's Sleep Problems*, *Dare to Discipline*, and *Raising Your Spirited Child* in one arm while Emily struggled and kicked on my hip, held fast by my other arm. The clerk glanced up, took in the vignette standing before her, and rang up the books without a word.

In the evenings, Mark would dash through the front door to swoop the girls into his arms. He invented games of chase that Emily loved to play while wearing a costume she called her "big, red dress." He got the idea to use crepe paper streamers to make the game more like a parade. The three of them would run through the house trailing long colored ribbons and giggling, our two daughters in dress-up clothes and their tall father in his scrubs. Most families have a fun parent.

One summer, when Emily was six, right before bedtime, she asked if we could pitch a tent and camp out in the yard. I immediately thought of several reasons to say no. It's late. The tent and sleeping bags are packed up in the basement. I'm tired. Before I could get the words out to nix the idea, Mark immediately agreed with Emily's plan, even though he had worked a full day. An hour later, Emily sat on Mark's lap while he read *Chrysanthemum* by flashlight in the tent just a few feet from our front door.

In middle school, Emily's life crumbled with Mark's terminal diagnosis. I had never been able to connect with her in the way her father had. Now she was stuck with me. Only me. Not the best me either.

Could it possibly get any more cliché? I was a tightly wound spool that had unraveled when my husband got cancer. After his funeral, choosing to continue the work of living was a daily decision influenced by the three beating hearts we had created together. Yet I had no idea how to recalculate this new existence because my brain was disoriented. I had been a full-time caretaker, my life consumed by the demands of that role, but it all came to a screeching halt beside an open grave. In January. In the freezing rain.

I had no job, structure, or initiative. Each day stretched before me, vast and empty. I didn't know what to do with myself to fill the hours. My phone was mostly silent, though I habitually checked the screen multiple times throughout the day for texts. Didn't anyone remember me or need me? I was adrift without my marital tether as I attempted to reach the surface of the life I used to know. It seemed to be somewhere above me, but my arms were too heavy to lift.

Mark's death opened an inlet port to some existential central vacuum inside me, and I felt as if my soul was being sucked out. All that remained was a hollow and rusted hull of my former life. I was acutely aware of being hugged by a tight sense of fragility and random tragedy. I stared into the ceiling at night, then struggled to heave myself from under the covers the next morning. I couldn't figure out how or why I was supposed to survive the wretchedness. Not knowing what else to do, I cried constantly, the wet tissues in my hand bearing tears of helplessness, fear, hopelessness, and grief as I tried to mechanically continue the routine of making meals, driving kids where they needed to go, and maintaining the household. Our children hid in their rooms or went to hang out at their friend's houses to avoid seeing their pathetic mother and listening to her cry. I understood why and that made me feel worse.

GETTING ANGRY

It's no secret that living with teenagers is often difficult, even when the circumstances are ideal. Which they certainly were not. Some days, I would get angry at Mark for dying (*how convenient!*) and leaving me alone to face this. He wasn't there to act as Switzerland, a neutral buffer zone where combatants could meet in peace. He wasn't there to translate what each of us really meant, as opposed to how the other party had mistakenly interpreted what we said or did. He wasn't there to comfort us when we were scratched and wounded by each other. He wasn't there to take over when I had reached my limit.

As every single parent knows, no one but you is standing between your child and the world. Others can help, yet most of the time, like the Farmer in the Dell's cheese, you stand alone. There is no division of labor, nor are there any days off. To do the job well requires superhuman wisdom, stoic patience, and Elastigirl's resilient flexibility. On a good day, I may have reflected a hint of one of these attributes, but good days were not the norm in that season of grief.

Leaving aside my capabilities for the task, I had three children looking to me to lead the way. I knew Mark counted on me to raise our children well because we discussed it. He did not express it this way, but I understood the character qualities he valued and would have wanted to pass on because he had exemplified them: generosity, candor, diligence, patience with others, and humility, to name a few. At first, I didn't fully grasp that this meant I had to model those traits myself, despite how I felt and regardless of being bewildered by grief and handicapped by a resulting depression.

In particular, I struggled to know how to do this regarding Emily. She refused to talk to anyone about her monumental loss but instead directed at me a conflagration of emotions she couldn't articulate. Having lost control of one parent, Emily seemed determined not to lose control of another. Nothing was too small for her to disagree about. Even the allusion of an opinion on my part would be challenged. We fought bitterly. As if there was not enough pain in our family, our epic conflicts created more. Her flippant, eye-rolling attitude was exhausting. Being a single mom to an angry, grieving teenage girl is like balancing on a high wire. Without a safety net. On a unicycle. With a flat tire.

One day, Emily texted me from school between classes. "Found kitten. Can I bring home?"

I texted back, "Only if you PROMISE to find it a home. Not keeping it!"

I later learned Emily's friend had found the kitten in the road on the way to school. The mother cat had been killed by a car. The kitten was only a few weeks old and in bad shape: dehydrated, flea-bitten, and suffering from an eye infection. We took the teeny creature to a veterinarian, who gently performed an examination.

"I'm not sure she's going to make it," he said, stroking the kitten's back. "We can certainly try, but I have to warn you. It will cost several hundred dollars, and she still might die."

He looked at me for an answer, and I looked at my daughter. She deliberately avoided my gaze. Her lips were pressed into a tight line, her fierce eyes slamming the door on unshed tears.

She stared at the wall. Knowing I would forever be labeled the "kitten killer" if I didn't say yes, I silently handed over my credit card. Half an hour and $500 later, we headed home. Emily held the kitten, and I held my tongue. A small paper bag containing eye ointment, skin salve, and antibiotics sat between us.

RISING TENSION AND A PIVOT POINT

From the start, I considered this kitten a foster pet. We already had two other cats; in my opinion, three tipped us into crazy cat-family territory. Despite the vet's odds, Foster Kitty thrived under Emily's loving nurture. She named her Scamp. When Emily was home, Scamp was her shadow, cuddling on her pillow at night and draping herself around Emily's neck as she did homework. Repeated trips to the vet were necessary for follow-up, flea treatments, vaccinations, and even minor surgery. Of course, since Emily was at school, the responsibility for arranging, carrying out, and paying for these vet appointments fell to me.

The free kitten was becoming increasingly time-consuming and expensive, though Emily did not appear to notice. I resented her lack of appreciation and assumption that I had adequate resources and nothing better to do than to chauffeur this cat. I dropped hints about finding it a forever home. These were ignored.

A few days after the kitten's latest vet visit, I was juggling bills at the kitchen table when Emily walked in and headed straight for the refrigerator. I looked over my glasses at her, feeling irritated about the kitten situation and tense due to the pile of bills. Rather than trying to talk with Emily about how she might help or even say hello to her, I aimed low.

"Your French teacher sent an email. Your last three homework assignments haven't been turned in," I said.

A minute passed. Silence.

"Did you hear me?" I asked.

"Yeah, I heard you," she said.

"Well . . ."

"Mom, I'll get to it."

"And when might that be, given that it's already overdue?" I said with a sarcastic edge.

"I *said* I'll get to it!" She banged the refrigerator door closed and glared at me.

"You *may not* talk to me that way!" I said indignantly, even though I had provoked her.

"Mom, why don't *you* leave me the hell alone?" she said, her voice rising.

Why? Because I was self-absorbed in my sadness and anger at everyone and everything, including Emily. She was a handy target for all of it. I snarled at her. "You're just a taker. You never contribute!" At last, I said what was bothering me, though my tone, timing, and lack of compassion were all way off.

"You think you do so much for me? Well, you *don't*. All my friends' moms do more than you do, and they do it better! You just sit around crying and feeling sorry for yourself."

In truth, she had that partly right. I did feel sorry for myself. I cried too easily and too often. But at that moment, she had wounded me, and all I could think about was getting even. Jumping to a stand, I charged up the stairs to Emily's room, where Scamp stayed.

"That's it! Scamp is out of here today! I am *done* doing nice things for you!"

I grabbed the kitten from Emily's bed before stomping back down the stairs into the living room, where she stood watching me.

Emily was not to be outmaneuvered. Spying my favorite cat, Leo, nestled on a nearby stuffed chair, she scooped him up before he could run away and then turned to face me. We stared at each other through hard, narrowed eyes, stuck in a classic standoff as we dangled our respective cats in front of us—like shields protecting our hearts. No more than ten feet between us, we were a million miles apart.

At that exact moment, the sun found a split in the clouds just outside the window. Celestial light flooded the room. The dramatic change pierced my anger, allowing for a humbling realization. Mark had been counting on me to make an extra effort to connect with Emily, knowing that our personalities were like plaids and stripes; they usually didn't go well together.

I took a deep breath, bent down, and gently put the kitten on the floor.

"Hey, isn't this ridiculous?" I asked, hoping Emily might see the humor in our catfight. She did not. Her hurt was too fresh. Dumping Leo on the chair, she turned her back on me and walked away, jaw tight and spine straight.

Though I didn't need one more reason to self-flagellate, now I had one. Instead of giving in, however, I resolved to do better. This was not the Hallmark channel, and there was no quick fix for our grief or anger. When my kids made a mistake, didn't I want them to learn from it, pick themselves back up, make adjustments or amends as necessary, and give it another go? I would be their example. First, I'd give Emily space before finding her to apologize.

CHAPTER 4
Do I have the courage to embrace what is strong and beautiful within me?

VIVA LAS VEGAS

Coach Rick strode a pace ahead, his broad shoulders and compact wrestler's form creating a wedge that parted other travelers. Several raised eyebrows and openly admiring stares were directed his way as I followed him down the airport concourse toward the iconic sign announcing, "Welcome to Las Vegas." No wonder. A bevy of ten attractive women in body-conscious outfits strode behind him, each of us exhibiting the results of our months and months of training. The following day, we would all compete in the Tri-Fitness World Challenge at the Monte Carlo Resort & Casino. Individually, we had overcome our demons, committed to self-discipline, and done the work to make this journey happen. As a group, we looked impressive.

Tri-Fitness is an athletic contest. Entrants select from a menu of physical challenges designed to test their fitness level against others their age. There's also a figure competition, which is somewhat like a toned-down version of a bodybuilding class. I had come to Las Vegas to compete in the figure portion of Tri-Fitness. Psychiatrists would point to certain childhood experiences to explain why I'd gotten involved.

As one of the ten women following Rick through the airport, I was part of this club. Yet I wore the mantle of its identity as one might a borrowed sweater, glad for the warmth but aware of its status as not truly my own. I'd first learned about Tri-Fitness only six months earlier. This made me the newest competitor on our team. I was also its oldest participant in a sport where youth is not a requirement yet definitely an asset. This experience was about testing my resolve to embrace life by doing something that felt simultaneously outrageous yet oddly affirming. I was about to show off my body in front of hundreds of people wearing only a rhinestone studded scrap of a bikini and four-inch-high Lucite heels. At age fifty-one.

HAVING BARBIE AS A ROLE MODEL

During my impressionable teenage years, my father said things like this:

"If you'd learn how to use makeup properly, it would probably help."

"You should practice how to walk gracefully. I married your mother because she was gorgeous, but she walked like a duck. I sent her to modeling school to learn how to walk."

"You need to marry young. Women lose their beauty and their influence as they age."

"Men get more powerful as they age; women just get older and look it."

"I want you to meet so-and-so's two daughters. You'll like them; they're both beautiful."

Other memorable father-daughter exchanges reinforced the overt message.

"Stand here," he said when I was a teenager, posing me next to the hood of his "good" car to take a few pictures. I knew the stereotype he was trying to emulate. I'd seen car advertisements featuring female models, but I was confused. He'd made it so clear that I didn't measure up in the looks department, and he rarely wanted a photo of me.

"Put your hand on the hood, look this way, and smile," he said.

I felt awkward and self-conscious, as if I was another possession to be cataloged. When I eventually saw the pictures, I detested them for revealing a stiff, unhappy young woman who was clearly out of her class compared to the beauty and elegance of his shiny Lincoln town car. Knowing that I didn't meet the standard my father envisioned, I was insecure about my appearance.

Then there was the dreaded "Spin around. I want to have a look at you." He'd usually say this instead of hello when he first saw me after a business trip, his index finger making a circle to demonstrate what he wanted. He would repeat the command more forcefully if I protested, indicating that refusal was not an option. Eyes down in embarrassment, I would do the twirl for him. He'd look me over head to toe, as one might when considering livestock for purchase.

"Hmmm, looks like you're putting on a bit of weight," he might say. Or "Have you thought about wearing your hair a different way? Pulling it off your face?"

Growing up, I concluded two things: first, physical appearance and beauty were of prime importance, and second, lack of compliments plus frequent criticism meant I wasn't good enough. Erasing this programming has been a lifelong struggle.

In my twenties, staying fit became an entrenched habit, if not a compulsion. It replaced the eating disorder I developed in college. The emotional roots of needing to control my body and look a certain way were not difficult to trace. The stories we create about ourselves in childhood can cast lifelong shadows. It's a crippling thing to believe that some fundamental flaw in the way you look is the reason for whatever dysfunction exists in your family of origin.

A CHANCE ENCOUNTER

After Mark died, going to the gym every morning was a means

of structuring the emptiness. Even if no one engaged me in conversation, I could at least be in the company of other people. The physical exertion gave me a way to release some of my sadness and anger.

Why him? Why us? Why me?

While I was working out on the weight machines, a trainer named Rick approached me. Taking off my headphones, I turned to face him, assuming he wanted to ask whether I'd move down the line a bit to give him more room.

"Hey, I see you here working out a lot. Would you consider upping your game? I think you'd be great for the grace and physique portion of the Women's Tri-Fitness Competition this summer. It's in Las Vegas."

I gave him a blank stare. Like most people, I had never heard of Tri-Fitness. What did he mean by competing in "grace and physique"? Rick pointed to a group of women about twenty feet away. He explained that he was training them for the competition and thought I might want to join the group. Glancing over, I saw five toned women in tight-fitting, Victoria's Secret-inspired workout outfits. They looked like cast members of *Charlie's Angels*. They were chatting and laughing as they warmed up. All of them were younger than me, some by just a few years, others by a lot more.

Me? With them?

Rick explained that Tri-Fitness is an athletic challenge that combines four events: completing a 180-foot Marine-style obstacle course, performing a dance-style fitness routine, doing timed fitness skills like repetitive bench pressing, and grace and physique. Athletes can participate in just one event, all events, or any combination. A level playing field is attempted by dividing participants into age groups. For me, that meant women over fifty. Competing in grace and physique involved walking across the stage and posing while wearing a competition bikini, high heels, and, of course, a smile.

Rick said my lean build and height made me an ideal candidate for grace and physique. He suggested that if I was interested, I should commit soon as there was "work to be done" to tone my body further and build more muscle. The competition was six months away.

I said I'd think about it.

At first, I was merely flattered by the compliment that someone thought I could do this. The idea of being on stage in a bikini, let alone at my age, was ludicrous. Wasn't it?

Then again, my entire adult life, I'd been obsessed with staying fit and maintaining my wedding day weight. For the past thirty-plus years, I had compulsively exercised and dieted to ensure that what was in my control was, in fact, controlled. The resulting self-discipline was a gift, a usable strength. Especially as I'd gotten older, I knew I stood out as one of the few moms able to swap jeans with my teenage daughters. When out and about, I still heard appreciative compliments from random strangers, men and women alike.

By suggesting I had what it took to compete in grace and physique, Rick unknowingly tapped into a psychological need to once again stand up to my father's discouraging assessments of me. How we remember and use our past has an essential motivational pull—a moon to the tide of our lives. Yes, I believed I could sculpt a stage-worthy body in six months.

Still, I hesitated. The people-pleasing part of me wondered, *What will others think*? I sought counsel from my girlfriends, expecting them to concur that doing the Tri-Fitness grace and physique competition was ridiculous. After all, most of them were church-going conservatives along the lines of "modest is hottest."

What I heard, however, were votes of encouragement and heartening support. This unexpected backing caused me to pause as I considered the what-ifs. I thought about Mark, my decision to do the motorcycle class, and my resolve to "live fully" through annual quests to honor his memory. What if the Tri-Fitness competition could be my challenge for the coming year?

The thought of competing was a daunting thing. The main obstacle was a variety of social fears: fear of embarrassment, fear of judgment, and fear of tripping and humiliating myself. The countervailing motivation was doing something in Mark's memory that would force me to acknowledge those fears and move ahead anyway.

Getting through grief was going to take time, but here dangled an opportunity to be brave like Mark while facing a different demon: insecurity about my looks. What woman in our culture doesn't attach value to her physical appearance? If Rick thought I could compete in grace and physique, that was enough for a start. Plus, as I did research and looked at the before and after photos of women close to my age who got in fabulous shape through intense weight training, I got excited to see what I could accomplish.

That evening, I called Rick to tell him I was in. He told me to be at the gym by 9 a.m.

TRAINING CAMP BEGINS

"Sweat like a pig to look like a fox" was printed on a card I taped to my bathroom mirror. The cartoon illustration of the two animals was humorous and cute. Reality, however, was an actual smelly, hot mess. By the time each daily training session was complete, my drenched hair would be plastered to my skull, my face would be red and blotchy, and my chest would be heaving as I squatted in a tripod position to catch my breath.

Why does anyone do such a thing? Clearly, the answer for each competitor is personal. For me, childhood insecurity was one component, but training for the competition also gave me a short-term goal to pursue. The company of the other Tri-Fitness women offered a small sense of connection. I was frequently lonely, still bogged down in grief and depression.

After almost two years of helping our family while Mark was sick, those closest to me needed to get back to their own lives. My friends had kids, jobs, and husbands and were busy navigating full agendas. They would call me on the go while rushing to complete their to-do lists, casually offering, "Let's meet up next week!" Often, other commitments intervened, or they forgot, not realizing how I was grasping for any opportunity to put something on my calendar. After sending our kids off to school, I'd be forced to consider what to do with myself for the next eight hours. My mental state caused me to have an inward focus that fed depression and sapped motivation. Continual reexamination of my circumstances led me further into unattractive self-pity. I moved through my days like the undead dead, hoping for some outside magic to jolt me back into a life I wanted to live, one where I felt purposeful and interacted with others.

Widowhood had unexpectedly revised my social landscape in other respects, too. Obviously, I no longer had Mark's daily companionship, but I hadn't previously considered how couples generally prefer the company of other couples. Including a single woman, or man, imbalances the dynamics. Additionally, the taint of spousal death is a significant downer. Anyone would pause before inviting the newly bereaved to an event designed for fun.

One of the benefits of preparing for Tri-Fitness was that it gave me a plan for the day, even if it was only completing the coach's workout. Over the ensuing weeks, I spent numerous hours lifting, running, and practicing. Lifting, running, and practicing. Day after day after day. Lifting, running, and practicing. Usually, I could set my mind on the workout and get it off my grief for a few hours. Plus, I often got to do my workouts alongside the others preparing for the competition.

There was an addictive positivity to this group of women.

I grabbed onto it with the desperate panic of a shopper on Christmas Eve, self-absorbed in filling my list of emotional needs. I'm embarrassed to admit that I also hoped for attention in the form of sympathy. This approach caused me to take a passive role during our group training sessions while I waited to see if anyone would initiate conversation or ask how I was doing.

Without fully understanding everything behind it, Rick simply noticed that I'd sit on the sidelines looking at the floor when it wasn't my turn to do whatever we were doing. Eventually, he pulled me aside.

"Look, you need to step it up. You're part of a team here. When you finish your set, I expect you to stay involved, encourage the other women, and cheer them on."

His comments threw cold water on my thinking. *Wait, I didn't get a hall pass as the grief-stricken newcomer?* No, I didn't. Get up. Leave the self-pity party. Help the others. Rick's words hit their mark. Regardless of how I felt, I needed to attempt to contribute.

That lesson's sting left a lasting impression on me. We've all heard that it's better to give than to receive. The reason relates to the orientation to self. Someone who wants to be on the receiving end is thinking of satisfying her needs. The person on the giving end is thinking about the needs of others. Rick was showing me the better way.

A TYPICAL SPIN CLASS, AN ATYPICAL RESPONSE

Where do cycle studios find those perky spin instructors, the ones with bionic stamina to smile and motivate the class as they do a grueling workout alongside us? These folk set the room's vibe. Using a combination of soft lighting and throbbing music, they cocoon and synchronize us, coaxing our legs to push and pull to the beat while they act as part cheerleader and part drill sergeant. We voluntarily place ourselves under their control, hoping to burn off our calories and our negative energy. For me, it's quite effective. And sometimes, quite painful.

A particular day stands out. In this class, we were led by one of my preferred instructors, a lean, fit dynamo sporting a black bandanna around her head. Four songs into it, we were dripping sweat despite the multiple fans aimed at us from every corner. Hard became harder as we added sprints, each one mini torture while we gave 100 percent to rotating the pedals as fast as we could for increasing intervals. During the fifteen-second rest between sets, I poured water into my mouth, letting it splash down my chin and onto my T-shirt. My pulse had barely slowed when Dynamo challenged us. "Turn it up!"

I leaned forward to give the dial an aggressive turn, significantly increasing the bike's resistance. If Dynamo could do it, so could I. Standing up to simulate a climb, I forcibly pressed my weight down on the pedals to get them to move. I commanded my legs to pedal in time to the pounding music and, within seconds, was straining to breathe. Lungs and quads screamed for me to quit. I would not. This was a test of will.

When the excruciating effort of maintaining speed began to flood all my senses, the dim lights gave me the freedom to mentally disassociate. Somehow, my legs kept pumping, but it was as though my skin had dissolved, removing the barrier between self and air. The music became my beating heart, and in the steady agony of pedaling on and on and on, my thoughts floated over fields of suffering, especially Mark's and mine. As I gasped for breath on the bike, I remembered how he, too, struggled to breathe while tumor secretions drowned his lungs. I remembered what we endured as we helplessly witnessed each other slide into separate divisions of hell while our children hovered on the sidelines, taking it all in without fully understanding the repercussions. Replaying these memories, my physical pain melted with my emotional pain until they were an indistinguishable blob, like crayons left to bake in the sun. My legs circled on.

Thinking of Mark, his death, our anguish, and the frightening prospect of trying to stand on my own without him, my chest began to heave. In that small, dark studio, with music blaring through speakers mounted in every corner, no one could tell that I had begun sobbing. Even though others were mere inches away on their bikes, I was mercifully alone.

A few minutes later, the workout was over. As Dynamo led us through a series of cool-down exercises, I gathered in my last tears. Closing my eyes to collect myself, I dug a towel out of my bag to clean my face, stretched, wiped down the bike, and left the gym. Having purged all that grief-tinged, tumultuous energy, a calmness followed me. The bike was stationary, but it moved me along in other ways.

THE DIET

I was considered "skinny fat." This sad description meant that despite my low body weight, certain parts still jiggled and had to be converted to lean muscle. Though generally careful about what I ate, I needed to overhaul my food intake to look the best on stage.

A figure competitor's strict, regimented, daily diet includes five to six mini meals. This may sound like a lot, but the second, fourth, and sixth meals are not *meals* as most people understand the term. They are 100-calorie snacks, like two cups of dry, raw spinach and just the white part of a single hard-boiled egg. The breakfast, lunch, and dinner meals consist of three components: a serving of lean meat the size of a deck of cards, half a small sweet potato, and one cup of steamed green vegetables. Period. Theoretically, you are eating every three to four hours, but the portions are pitiful and miserly. Some competitors need to drop twenty to thirty pounds to get ready.

We live in a culture where food and food messages are ubiquitous. Our social interactions revolve around food. Choosing to endure gnawing hunger is an ascetic mindset that sets Tri-Fitness athletes apart and can make others uncomfortably aware of their own eating. Iron fortitude is required to stick to this diet. Serious competitors spend their days carrying coolers filled with celery, packets of mustard, and containers holding a few bites of fish and cooked green vegetables, usually asparagus. Asparagus is thought to be a diuretic that eliminates water from the body. Being slightly dehydrated helps display the "cut" of the individual's muscles on stage, which means the judges can see the clear separation between muscle groups.

Since this competition would be my first and last, I didn't get a portable cooler. I paid homage to the diet by making different choices, eating more frequent small meals, and keeping to the recommended clean foods list. I never eliminated carbs or gave up an occasional glass of wine. My hunger wasn't a significant distraction, thanks to an undercurrent of grief and depression.

Doing Tri-Fitness was primarily about having a short-term goal and trying something new. For others in our group, it was a lifestyle. They built practice obstacle courses in their backyards, invested in home gyms with mirror-lined walls, and attended training camps. They were willing to share tips on what they had learned, but nothing could replace their years of experience.

LEARNING TO WALK

Our team worked with a local choreographer, a talented man named Kevin, to coach us on the walking sequence for our onstage solos. We gathered in a mirrored studio at the gym for our first practice session. Kevin's upbeat flamboyance was contagious. When he first demonstrated how we were to walk, he exaggerated his movements the way a kindergarten teacher does when trying to show the little ones what to do. Though we smiled at Kevin's grandiose, swept arm sashay, we took serious note of all the steps that went into it. What seemed to be a simple thing, a minute and a half to cross a stage interspersed with three specific stops for posing, was not simple at all. Those ninety seconds would be a performance, a one-time distilled chance to put our training and dieting on display. Every body part needed to do its bit to enhance the overall presentation.

When we paraded before the judges, Kevin instructed that our goal would be to do all of the following. Hold your stomach in and your chest up. Rotate your torso sideways a la "Walk Like an Egyptian," as you gracefully step forward—on four-inch stiletto heels, no less. (Though it might feel awkward, turning this way highlights the chisel of your waist.) Carry your arms slightly away from your body, Barbie style. Make sure you look poised at all times. When you reach center stage, pause, look the panel of judges in the eye, and put on your most dazzling smile. Then strike your first pose.

Posing offers the chance to show off your best features. A typical pose involves a T-stance with one leg in front of the other and one or both arms on your hips. Kevin demonstrated.

We each tried to copy him, our reflections forming a ragged chorus line in the studio mirror. He showed us how to hold this first pose for a few seconds, smile, and again make eye contact with the judges. Next, we stepped forward, pivoting on our lead foot until we had turned to display our backs and booty. Here, we struck a second pose. After a pause, we were to turn 180 degrees to face forward once more and then immediately walk to the left side of the stage to do the same pause and pose sequence a final time before exiting.

Like so many seemingly simple acts, it was much harder than it looked. For one thing, to practice effectively required wearing a pair of competition shoes, clear Lucite extra high, high heels that visually elongated your legs. Walking gracefully in such footwear was a skill to be learned.

Practice attire included short shorts and a tank top to ensure that your form was visible. The studio mirror offered ample feedback as well as additional motivation to those who needed to be more diligent with dieting. As each of us took turns, Kevin and the others also chimed in with suggestions. This wasn't done in a catty way but with the intent to improve. Were you flexing your muscles to advantage? Did your arms need to be held a different way? Did you need to arch your back more or perhaps less?

The first time I attempted the walking-posing routine, my shoe caught on the carpet, and I stumbled. "That's okay," Kevin encouraged, "just keep going." The other women nodded sympathetically. My cheeks burned as I finished the short routine. Kevin reassured all of us. "The competition stage has a hard surface. That will make it easier to walk. Just remember to pick your feet up."

Watching everyone else do the same routine gave me a visual. I could see the pacing and posture that looked the most graceful and poised. Details like the position of your index finger or whether you put your hand on your hip made a difference. These were things I could work on. What I couldn't change was being ten years older than the next oldest woman in our group. As an "over fifty" competitor, I was already at the top of the age categories. All the more reason to fully enjoy the process while not taking it too seriously. No one would remember me ten minutes after the competition—so long as I didn't trip on stage.

Kevin played music to get us in the groove while we practiced. One of my favorite songs was by Bruno Mars. It seemed tailor-made to encourage a confident strut with its boogie drumbeat, quick tempo, and uplifting refrain—"Girl, you're amazing, just the way you are." Years later, hearing this song still puts me in the mood to begin a deliberate yet jaunty walk across an imaginary stage.

Being a visitor to this world of figure competition gave me an insider's view so I could appreciate who did it and why, respect their iron discipline, and even improve my physique and self-confidence. As a mere dilettante, however, I recognized that I hadn't found a long-term purpose or tribe. Competing in Tri-Fitness would give just enough battery charge to my life to last until I could find another temporary docking station. At the time, this was sufficient.

LIGHTS, CAMERA, ACTION

The Tri-Fitness World Competition took place on the Las Vegas Strip at the Monte Carlo Resort & Casino. We checked in on Thursday. Grace and physique was held on the stage of the Lance Burton Theater on Friday. Those of us from Lancaster decided to bunk up together to save money. I shared a double, optimistically described as "deluxe," with three others.

Our room's teeny bathroom could barely accommodate two at the mirror. Getting ourselves bikini-ready the following morning was a messy dance quartet involving scheduled shower times, tense performers, and an obstacle course of strewn clothing, suitcases, makeup, and shoes. We all overpacked. Every beauty implement known to modern womanhood was included in at least one person's suitcase. "Does anyone have..?" Fill in the blank—whitening strips, boob tape, hair spray, depilatory cream, eyelash glue, cuticle scissors, or some other necessity. Among the four of us, someone had it.

An enterprising pair of entrepreneurs, friends of some competitors, had set up a spray tanning operation in the bathtub of a guest room on the fourth floor. They had furtively stood near the Tri-Fitness registration table the previous day, passing out handwritten flyers to advertise their services while trying to avoid drawing the notice of Monte Carlo staff. Undoubtedly, the hotel would have put a quick end to this business with its potential to recolor the walls. My roommates and I signed up for back-to-back slots on the morning of grace and physique. One of the operators warned us to arrive separately, bring a shower cap, and keep the noise down.

Having showered and dried my hair, I gently knocked on the door of the bootleg spray tanning operation at 9:15 a.m., a few hours before the competition. A young woman wearing a silky wrap robe, her head in a towel, let me inside. We walked past the bathroom, where I could see plastic sheeting duct-taped to the walls, two people at work spraying a third person, a counter full of bottles, and a portable spray tan machine the size of a canister vacuum.

Entering the confined bedroom area was like being enveloped in a sorority party. A dozen women talked, laughed, and shared crudité while in various stages of undress. Everyone waited, whether to get sprayed or for their tans to dry, while they lounged on the beds or the floor. Within minutes, I was pulled into a lively conversation about the events I had signed up for and my training.

"Jennifer!"

My name was called from the direction of the bathroom. As I moved toward it, Tina, one of the tanning operators, leaned out of the doorway to hand me a paper thong bikini the size of a two-cup coffee filter.

"Here, put this on," she said. "You're next."

I stepped into the bathroom and squeezed behind the door. Flattened against the wall, I slipped out of my T-shirt and gym shorts, then stuffed my hair into a shower cap before putting on the disposable scrap of paper and string. The ridiculous thong was all that stood between me and total nudity. My butt's dimpled flesh had nowhere to hide. A few weeks earlier, I'd asked one of the other women who trained with our group what she did about stubborn posterior cellulite.

"I tan the hell out of it," she said.

With my arms crossed, I emerged from behind the door. Intent on their work, I was simply another pale canvas to Tina and her partner Ashley. Neither woman looked up. Whatever thoughts they had about seeing scores of practically naked female shapes, they kept to themselves.

"Okay, if you're ready, stand in the shower with your arms above your head."

Feeling self-conscious, I nonetheless did as told. A damp towel had been laid on the shower floor to prevent the tanning solution from being absorbed by the soles of my feet. It felt cold and squishy as I stepped onto it. In response to direction, I turned like a chicken on a spit as Ashley sprayed my Cheerio-colored skin a gorgeous honey tan, giving extra color to the aforementioned rear bumper at my request.

When the job was complete, I was taken aback by the transformation I saw in the mirror. The effect was instant. My physique seemed to look better, even to me, a fair-skinned redhead who had never had a tan in her entire life. Studies of the effect of tanning on attractiveness levels corroborate this phenomenon. Tan skin is considered more appealing. Moreover, my chameleon-like color change felt like an added layer of disguise. Hiding under my tan would help me create an alter ego for myself. I could play a woman with the confidence to rock that shimmery aqua-blue bikini I'd be wearing.

Once tanned, I returned to our shared room to put on makeup and finish getting ready. One more hour until we were due in the theater for the lineup. At the thought of walking across the stage in my bikini, it felt like tiny fluffy kittens were scampering across my midsection. There was no one to reassure me; everyone else was attending to their preparations. *Breathe*, I told myself.

I waited until the last fifteen minutes to put on my two-piece costume. This was deliberate. I needed to eliminate all traces of the coffee I'd had earlier. Getting into that bikini was a point of no return regarding comfort and convenience. The reason is a practical one, and its name is "butt glue."

My roommates introduced me to this product specifically designed to keep everything in place during the walking and posing segments of a beauty or fitness competition. Given the teeny amount of fabric involved, butt glue was essential to ensure that the material, such as it was, firmly adhered to my skin so it would not migrate. Of course, once the glue is applied, the bikini is semi-permanently "on" for the next several hours. Consider this carefully if you are someone like me whose nerves require repeated trips to the bathroom.

When we assembled backstage at the designated time, I counted eight in the "over fifty" class. Each of us wore a number pinned near our hip so the judges could score us for style, musculature, symmetry, and grace of movement. Every aspect of our performance would be observed and evaluated. Being women, we silently did this among ourselves, too, our eyes calculating our chances compared to those around us.

Glancing over my competition, I mentally picked out who I thought would win: a woman in a seashell-pink bikini sprinkled with eye-catching crystals. She stood out for her tall elegance, sculptured physique, and side-swept golden hair falling in soft waves below her shoulders. She certainly didn't look over fifty. Surely, she was someone who knew firsthand that one of the costs of being strikingly beautiful was the jealousy she aroused in others of her sex.

Somebody with a clipboard motioned for us to stand a few feet offstage, arranging us by height, so I was second to last, right next to Pink Bikini at the end of the line. She whispered to me how nervous she was. Though I'd been intimidated by her dazzling good looks, her confession forged a brief connection.

We exchanged smiles but didn't get to talk for long. The event organizers needed to keep the show running. I heard our class announced, and then the line began moving forward one by one, reminding me of a rookery of penguins, each waiting to take its turn to jump into frigid waters. In no time, the person holding the clipboard tapped me on the shoulder, "Number forty-five, go!"

I emerged from the curtain's protection into the blinding glare of the stage lights. The theater was only half filled, the seats occupied by other competitors, coaches, family, friends, and curious onlookers. It didn't matter because my nervousness wasn't tied to the number of spectators but to the fact that I was on display. In a rhinestone-studded bikini. And four-inch high heels. Five judges stared at me from their seats in the front row.

Instead of panicking, my brain went into protective mode by simply disconnecting conscious thought from the rest of my body. Fortunately, my alter ego took command without hesitation, confidently remembered what to do, and easily performed the walking and posing routine without a single misstep.

From their side-stage view, my teammates watched, poking each other and smiling because, apparently, I nailed it. Later, one shared with me, "We wondered where you've been hiding those gorgeous quad muscles. You looked amazing." This was high praise, especially from one of our group's more experienced women.

After each of us had completed our walk, the entire company of "over fifty" competitors passed across the stage in a long parade to cheers and applause. When the results were announced, I heard my name called as the first-place winner for our class.

What?

This plot twist surprised me. The Lancaster contingent whooped and cheered as I received the gold medal. No one saw my inner child shadowing me to the podium while silently wondering what my dad would think. Though he had died a few years earlier, his hold on my self-image was as tenacious as any other childhood indoctrination. Like many people, I chose to push back against my father's limiting beliefs, but they were a programming bug I could never fully erase. Fortunately, the yin of a parent's negative opinion is sometimes counterbalanced by the yang of achievement.

THE ROCKING CHAIR TEST

When I'd first considered doing Tri-Fitness, I asked myself which would be the bigger regret: possibly embarrassing myself by going on stage in a bikini or wondering down the road, perhaps as an eighty-year-old sitting on a rocking chair, what might have happened. When I look back over my life, do I want my choices and memories to reflect that I preferred sticking to what I knew or that I accepted appropriate risks and tested my courage? I concluded that I'd rather laugh over an epic failure than be someone with no stories to tell.

Living fully requires action. Instead of adopting the safe, expected route, could I spice up my life by adding daring new experiences? Whenever my life's script could be upgraded to include something different or exciting that forced me to take a chance, I needed to say yes. Moving forward, I was determined to do at least one challenging activity, event, or undertaking every year. Since Mark was no longer physically in front of me to point the way, I had to plot my own course. Without realizing it, I'd lit a candle to help me find a way through the cavernous black tunnel called grief.

The problem was that short-term goals like doing Tri-Fitness did not provide a long-term solution to the fundamental crisis I was having. *What am I supposed to do with my life now?* I needed a new purpose to refashion my future, something I could throw myself into with the same enthusiasm as helping and caring for Mark. Yet, countervailing that need was the static of managing my grief, a daily chore that left me wrung out—flat as a load of rags that needed to be peeled off the washing machine drum. Coming up with a life purpose would have to wait. I was still recovering from the tragedy of what had happened to our family, and I still thought of myself as the surviving half of a couple. Of course I did. Mark had only been gone a year.

CHAPTER 5

Can I take my own physical pain and use it in honor of Mark and in recognition of what he endured?

MILES TO GO, PROMISES TO KEEP

Before getting sick, Mark did things like the annual 4.4-mile open water swim across the Chesapeake Bay and a three-day, 200-mile bike ride through the mountains of Pennsylvania. Then, the disease stepped in and pummeled him. Seeing how cancer chipped away at my husband was like watching a lumberjack take an axe to a great oak.

He lost weight, hair, and feeling in his fingers and toes. We went from biking together to walking together. We'd go around the neighborhood, then just around the block, then only to the end of the driveway. Eventually, our walks slowed to a shuffle. We took shuffling walks for shorter and shorter distances until all he could manage was pushing a walker around the circle from the kitchen to the dining room to the living room. In the end, the outcome was no surprise. The oak fell. His fortitude kept him alive a year longer than had been predicted.

Experts say that when life is stressful, sticking to a daily routine is one way to cope. Unfortunately, after Mark died, the full-time caregiving that had occupied me during his illness was no longer necessary. I had no routine and didn't know what to do with myself. Once the Tri-Fitness competition ended, an uncharacteristic passivity crossed my threshold and dropped its heavy cloak on my shoulders. Deep depression slithered in just behind, and for added measure, loneliness once again tripped the power switch.

These uninvited leeches hooked on tenaciously, leaving me with little energy to reach out to others or make long-term plans like returning to work. After a few unsuccessful attempts to be social, I discovered I'd lost the resilience for even the smallest rejection. A friend too busy to meet for lunch had a disproportionately negative effect on my mental status. As before, going to the gym was sometimes the only reason to leave the house.

One morning in December, while swiping my card at the check-in desk, I saw a stack of flyers for an organization called Team in Training, or TNT, sitting on the counter. Alongside a photo of smiling cyclists was the headline "Participate. Move. Raise. Cure" and something about beating cancer to the finish line.

The Leukemia & Lymphoma Society (LLS) was formed to find cures for blood cancers like leukemia, myeloma, lymphoma, and Hodgkin's. TNT uses endurance sports such as triathlons, marathons, and century (100-mile) cycling events to raise money for LLS. Athlete participants solicit sponsors to make a donation per event or mile completed. TNT offers coaching to help prepare athletes for the events by providing daily workout plans, group training, and administrative support for fundraising.

After reviewing the flyer, I attended a local presentation on LLS's work to eradicate blood cancers. While watching an inspiring video showing athletes and cheering supporters, I considered doing a TNT cycling event as my next legacy challenge in Mark's memory. My initial concern was not about the 100-mile distance or attempting to do this at age fifty-two but about the required fundraising. The TNT representative explained that we each needed to raise $4,000 in sponsorships to participate. Hearing this number, I crossed my arms and leaned back in the folding chair. My attitude changed, however, when the event date was announced: June 7 of the coming year. Had Mark lived, June 7 would have been our twenty-second wedding anniversary.

Although he had not had blood cancer, I figured that any cancer research could ultimately benefit other types. It was simple. Helping LLS would be pro-research and anti-cancer. That was my camp, too. The event date clinched my decision. I left the meeting with high hopes and a folder of information. I would have five months to reach my fundraising goal and prepare to cycle 100 miles in a single day over the hilly roads that circumnavigate Lake Tahoe.

Shortly thereafter, I recruited my sister-in-law, Perri, to do the ride with me. She lived over an hour away, so we rarely got to ride together. She went online to look at the course, checked the dates to ensure they would work for her schedule, and signed up. Her presence added another layer of support and fun to this adventure.

TNT training began a few weeks later, at the end of January. Altogether, there were fourteen cyclists from the Central Pennsylvania region who had committed to doing Tahoe. As part of the training, we each were given a ride schedule of suggested goals for the eighteen weeks of training. Each of us would be expected to put in at least 1,500 miles of riding before Tahoe, beginning with thirty-five miles as the longest ride of the week, then eventually working up to completing a sixty-mile ride just before the event. Our head coach organized regular team rides where we could cycle together as a group. Those who couldn't attend the group rides were expected to put in the distance independently.

Pennsylvania winters never paired well with biking. Daylight faded by 4:30 p.m., temperatures barely reached forty degrees, and the wind felt miserable as it tried to blow us backward while we pedaled over the frozen landscape. Despite multiple layers, fingers and toes were swollen, blue, and numb once the day's ride was completed. Many on our team, like me, were riding in honor or memory of someone who had cancer. Pushing through the ordeal of training allowed us to symbolically feel a small bit of what they felt.

Of course, once our miles were completed for the day, we got to dismount, go out for food and drinks, and enjoy the camaraderie of being tired but satisfied. Each week, we went further and got stronger. It was the reverse of watching my husband live with cancer.

Mark had been an athlete throughout his life. He used endurance sports as an outlet that allowed him to stay focused during long hours at work despite his kinesthetic restlessness. Metastatic cancer hijacked his body. He could not wrestle the reins from this enemy and force his way back to safety. He had to live with the knowledge that his cells were betraying him and doing so with increasing force and velocity. By contrast, throughout his illness, my flesh had the audacity to be healthy. My cells were doing what cells ought to do, not haphazardly refusing to adhere to their predetermined life cycle and going *Terminator*. Watching someone you love succumb to cancer is to face the ugly reality that you cannot share their mortal pain, only witness it.

My decision to ride, to endure a chosen pain, was not an atonement, only an acknowledgment and a way to honor his life. It was my way to face a different version of torment in solidarity with Mark even though his suffering was now over. This is what humans do. We reenact to remember.

THE DEPLORABLE QUESTION

By April, the weather was finally giving us a break. One Saturday, I joined a training ride that included several people I had not yet met. We were bicycling through the hilly farmland around the quaint town of Strasburg, once voted one of America's ten most historic and picturesque towns. Evening was settling in. The birds were calling back and forth, creating a soft cacophony of twittering in the background. The country roads were devoid of cars. Green pastures nourished herds of dairy cows, and newly plowed fields awaited seed.

Despite the idyllic setting, my body felt tired and hungry. My mind ordered my legs to keep pumping, but my legs were talking back like rebellious teenagers. Another woman I didn't know pedaled beside me.

"I heard that you are riding Tahoe in your husband's memory," she said.

"That's right."

"What kind of cancer did he have?"

"Stomach cancer."

"He must have gone fast," she said.

Caught off guard by this blunt observation, I stopped pedaling. The bike continued to coast, and I could hear the ratchet in the rear hub clicking like a repetitive, admonishing "tsk, tsk, tsk."

"He lived nineteen months after his diagnosis," I said.

She had another question. "How was his quality of life during those nineteen months?"

I gripped the handlebars tighter and clenched my jaw. Clearly, Miss Sensitivity hadn't lost anyone to a terminal illness. How was she supposed to know how to tiptoe gently? Still, what she asked wasn't the sort of thing you'd share with a stranger.

For the uninitiated, a cancer journey might not look so bad when you see it in the movies or on TV because it's condensed and sanitized. In reality, there is a lot of long, drawn-out suffering. How was his quality of life? What was it this woman wanted to know? Mark had been cast as the lead actor in a tragedy involving a stage 4 cancer diagnosis. As a physician, he'd read the script and knew how it would end. He'd had to look into the pained eyes of everyone who loved him, knowing he was at the heart of their suffering. Add to that living through the brutality of the disease and its equally brutal treatments, which caused exhaustion that he said felt like its own mini-death. He endured all this while attempting to maintain hope. He did that part for us. He fought longer than he wanted to out of love for his children and me.

During this time, Mark and I each drifted on our fragile canoes of personal isolation. Despite a community of support that nurtured, cared for, fed, and prayed over us, no one could volunteer to remove the feelings of powerlessness (his) or terror (mine) that accompanied the knowledge that he was going to die. We reached a tacit agreement in which we tried to shield each other by stoically holding it together and not voicing our worst fears. We played this charade as if doing so could put off reality. Instead of venting to me, Mark and our church pastor would go into the study and shut the door, emerging red-eyed an hour later. I would go for a drive to call my brother, sister, or friend and sob over the phone.

We had hoped for God to give us one show-stopping miraculous cure. Instead, we saw small signs that offered heavenly reassurance as Mark slipped closer to the grave. These were the last days of us getting to be a whole family. There is a gift in getting the opportunity to prepare for death, say goodbye, and offer all of yourself so that your role in the last chapter of your loved one's life reflects what you want it to be. We squeezed out every possible bit of joy and infused it with as much love as we could. We rose to the occasion and fell to our knees. It was what we were given but not what we wanted to receive.

Thinking of all this in response to the question about Mark's quality of life, I wanted to slide off the bike, wrap my arms around my knees, squeeze my eyes shut, and rock while emitting a guttural, howling sound. But I didn't. Instead, I merely slowed my pace and dropped back. I pedaled listlessly, the painfully slow momentum of my legs reflecting the level of my spirit. The solidarity I usually enjoyed while in the company of TNT folks had gone ahead without me. Struggling at the back of the pack the last few miles, I couldn't wait to be done—off the bike and into the warm refuge of my car. After reaching it, I made excuses for not going out with everyone for food, loaded my bike in the trunk, and then sat staring at nothing until I felt the oscillations of grief dissipate and finally stop.

ALL ABOUT THE MONEY

I had been making steady progress toward the $4,000 fundraising goal. My only appeal had been to send out a letter describing the bike ride, my motivation to do it in Mark's memory, and requesting support. It was a well-written letter for those who took the time to read it, but the letter was not what caused people to respond. Mark himself was the reason. Mark helped thousands as a dermatologic surgeon, made us laugh by mimicking sounds and people and dialects, dressed as Moses to teach first-grade Sunday School, and invariably noticed whatever was humorous in a given situation. He was someone who healed, led, reassured, taught, fixed, could befriend just about anyone, and loved well.

I sent the letter to every person who had attended Mark's funeral, anyone who sent me a card during his illness, a lot of his medical colleagues, most of my extended family, and whoever else I thought might be even remotely interested. Checks for five, ten, and twenty dollars trickled in, with an occasional fifty or hundred here and there. I wrote a personal thank-you to each donor regardless of the amount, not wishing to be someone who solicits, gets a donation, and is not heard from again until their next solicitation.

Three weeks before the fundraising deadline, I was still $800 short of raising the necessary $4,000. Miraculously, a high school classmate who had heard of my effort through a mutual friend surprised me with a $1,000 donation. His extreme generosity pushed me over the minimum. My spot at the starting line in Tahoe was assured.

RACE DAY

My alarm was set for 4:15 on race day morning, but my eyes snapped open at 4:07 a.m. Perri and I had ordered two pots of coffee from room service. When they arrived, the pre-ride jitters had already taken hold. We were so jacked up that caffeine was unnecessary. We barely touched it.

The ride began in South Lake Tahoe, Nevada, a resort town in the Sierra Nevada mountains. Our 100-mile loop would go clockwise around the lake from there. In the adrenaline rush of being with thousands of other cyclists, I didn't even notice the lower oxygen levels that went with being at a higher elevation.

The previous day had been rainy, with temperatures in the low forties. Now, not sure what to wear or bring to the starting line, I put on three layers. My pockets bulged with power bars, Gatorade packets, Kleenex, ibuprofen, a camera, and my cell phone. Hoping I hadn't forgotten anything important, we scrambled into the hall. The carpeted corridor was quiet except for our bikes' clicking sound as we walked toward the elevator. On the door of each room housing a team member, our coach had taped a sign: "A Hero Sleeps Here."

Due to the logistics of getting the 600 cyclists who stayed in our hotel along with their bicycles down the limited number of elevators, we'd been instructed to avoid the rush by bringing our bikes to the lobby at 4:30 a.m. The doors opened to a gathering carnival when we reached the ground floor. Coach was looking for us and directed Perri and me to a side section of the lobby. Sitting on the floor next to our gear, we shared hot chocolate in Styrofoam cups. Despite the smiles, a pre-ride tension electrified these moments. Then Hubert, our team's lead jokester, showed up late (as always), having dyed his beard and hair TNT's signature color—bright purple. Without saying a word, Hubert reminded me that I was here to have fun.

Meanwhile, other TNT teams from around the country were assembling. According to tradition, each team had attached an ornament unique to its region of the country to their cycling helmets. The helmet decorations reflected humor and creativity, many of them involving food. I saw cows on surfboards, plastic wine glasses filled with fake grapes, small inflatable flamingos, model airplanes manned by tiny dolls, energizer bunnies carrying drums, ears of corn, and spam cans. Our team wore oversized, stuffed toy Hershey Kisses. The decorations added to the party atmosphere and made it easy to locate fellow teammates. We took group photos and then headed to the starting line.

As we lined up, the mountains were awakening, blushing with thoughts of the coming sun. We had all dressed on the light side, knowing that once the ride got going, we would be peeling off our extra layers. Meanwhile, we stood around with our breath visible in the chilly mountain air. The crowd buzzed like a hive, each rider intent on last-minute tasks: checking tire pressures, sharing power bars, taking more photos, and running back into the lobby for a final trip to the bathroom. Excitement braided with nervousness at the thought that hours and hours of training were about to be tested. Perri and I looked at each other. Conversation took the form of raised eyebrows and pursed lips since there wasn't much to say at this point.

Multiple teams lined up in front of and behind us. At 6 a.m. sharp, the mayor of South Lake Tahoe appeared, welcomed us all, and gave a safety speech. Was anyone really listening? Next, the ride organizer had us sing "The Star-Spangled Banner" as we stood in the dawn's early light. A short while later, an official dropped a flag, and the ride began.

We started with a crash, literally. The first twenty-five feet of the course required hundreds of riders to make a sharp ninety-degree turn out of the parking lot and onto the road. One of my teammates turned too sharply and fell, taking down several other riders. We came to learn at the end of the ride that she had sustained a hairline fracture in her leg. At first, not realizing she'd done so, she picked herself up and took off but was forced to quit riding at mile forty-eight when the pain became intolerable.

Eventually, 3,100 pairs of pumping legs would cross the starting line to begin this journey. After the first quarter mile, the pack thinned so we could space ourselves out. Perri and I were riding side by side. We left the main drag of South Lake Tahoe at a steady clip, my odometer registering 19 mph. Morning cold penetrated my cycling jacket and TNT jersey; the only sounds were the shifting of gears, the hum of skinny tires on pavement, the wind in my ears, and hearing "left" or "on your left" as pelotons whipped by with mere inches to spare. We cruised on a flat road, our anxious energy finally having an outlet.

We hit our first climb at mile eleven. Just before the ascent began, Perri and I pulled over to "drop trou" behind some ten-foot boulders that provided cover. Suffice it to say, I ended up with pine needles in my bike shorts. Perri laughingly reminded me of a similar incident the year before involving stickle burrs. Despite this discomfort, months of training paid off as I passed rider after rider on this initial climb. I caught Hubert, who had apparently ridden past us while we squatted behind the boulder. He stood on his pedals, puffing hard as he worked the hill. To distract him, I mentioned the pine needle problem. Between breaths, he kindly offered to remove them personally. I declined.

By the time we crested the Inspiration Point overlook, dawn

had become morning. We could see across Emerald Bay with its signature mini island, but we were still so early into the ride that the stunning scenery took a backseat to the business of covering miles. Perri and I positioned ourselves low on the bike frame as we began the long, steep descent, our chins inches from the handlebars. The evergreens on either side of us blurred into a wall of green as we plunged downhill, gaining speed. I knew my odometer's numbers were ticking upward, but hurtling down a mountain at high speed while balancing on skinny racing tires requires total concentration. Hitting a small patch of road debris or even a stray pebble can cause a rider to skid and crash, resulting in serious bodily injury or death. At 37 mph, my appetite for risk maxed out so I lightly pulled on both brakes. More daring riders later reported exceeding 50 mph on this descent, a freakishly fast speed on a bicycle.

Our next segment included the "Truckee loop." This is an out-and-back ride to the nearby town of Truckee for the sole purpose of adding mileage. The first part of the loop is on an eight-foot-wide, off-road bike path alongside a creek so clear and shallow that you could see the rock-strewn bottom. The creek itself evidenced the power of collective effort. In the same way that each small rivulet had contributed to the stream, each of us who rode for TNT knew that our collectiveness made an impact. Together, our fundraising efforts had pooled to form a river that was $6.8 million strong.

We each rode for our own reasons. For some, the cause was noble but remote to their own lives. Their fight pitted them against the course, their previous times, and even against each other in a battle of determination and grit. For these riders, this was a battle of physical strength. For others, like me, this ride was a personal war against a disease that had savagely robbed us, ripping away our security or crushing some of us beneath memories tied to words most people never want to become familiar with—oncology units, chemotherapy, tumor scans, IV infusion, salvage therapy, and hospice, to name a few.

As we rode, we had an emotional component strapped onto our hearts. We fought the distance and the climbs with a fierceness reserved for mortal enemies. Remembering our cancer journeys, we rejoiced to finish our race even as we honored those who had fought until the very end of theirs. Riding for TNT gave us a venue to fight against cancer, fear, and despair.

This was not a flat, easy ride. The 100-mile distance was punishing in and of itself, even before you considered the hills. There's an overall elevation gain of 4,407 feet, which roughly translates to four times the height of the Empire State Building. Then, just before mile eighty, riders are confronted with the infamous seven-mile climb known as "Spooner," named after the small lake near the top. This extended ascent involves an elevation gain comparable to a 100-story building (1,060 feet), not too bad except that having already covered a distance equivalent to riding from New York City to Philadelphia, most riders are nearly ready to call it quits. That's when this little hill begins.

About three-quarters of the way up Spooner, the muscles between my shoulders were on fire, my legs were throbbing with each rotation of the pedals, my butt was numb, and I was panting hard. The sun beat down mercilessly, heating the asphalt and filling my nostrils with the pungent smell of tar. Ahead of me, for as far as I could see, the road continued to angle upward. My tank was empty from the sustained effort of the eighty-five miles I had already flattened under my tires.

My brain weighed the options. To keep going meant enduring more pain, yet to stop pedaling meant I'd immediately topple sideways and slam down on the road since my shoes were clipped onto the bike. Neither choice was attractive, but at least I got to choose. Mark never had a choice.

Even as we tried to deny it, we had known he would die, and

I would have to survive alone. I remember how his eyes lingered on our children, aware that he would never see them grow up. Unable to step aside, we watched death approach, each of us silently wondering about my ability to carry on without him. Now here I was. I didn't *have* to ride; I *got* to ride.

Leaning over the handlebars while sucking in air, I thought about all those who had donated toward my ride. As a distraction, I counted the riders I passed who were worse off than me—or at least slower. Many were walking their bikes. That's not to say that I wasn't getting passed myself. I was. It didn't matter. This was not a race; everyone was simply doing his or her best to complete all 100 miles. After passing the forty-seventh rider, one for each year of Mark's life, I stopped counting. Shortly thereafter, I reached the top.

Finishing all seven miles of that hill was a physical triumph. After turning into the small parking lot, I saw several of my teammates and wobbled toward them. My limbs were thick with lactic acid; I clumsily dismounted, but my legs refused to hold me. Someone caught me and eased me to the ground. A few minutes passed before I could come to a creaky stand. Perri arrived not long after.

We broke into huge smiles, hugged, and cheered. From the peak of Spooner, it's a mere twelve miles, mostly downhill, to the finish line. Having made it that far, completing the ride was virtually guaranteed. We sipped water and downed one last power bar. After snapping a few photos, we remounted our bikes.

Lake Tahoe sat to our right as we descended the back side of Spooner. I remember blue-green water pinned to the rocky shore by giant boulders. Pine trees and scrubby underbrush dug into the steep hillsides which waded into the lake's shallows. All of it flashed by in seconds as we gained speed. The bicycle sounds of humming tires, clicking gears, and rotating pedals were now so familiar that I had to focus just to hear them. No one passed us. A combination of exhilaration, grief, Mark's memory, and determination kicked in. I hammered out those last twelve miles, feeling so strong that I surprised myself. Did I only imagine Mark's hand on the small of my back pushing me along as he had when we'd met cycling twenty-six years earlier? I felt self-conscious then, wondering about the man whose help I needed to get home on a broken bike. Now that same man was still helping me, not by pushing but by inspiring through his example.

I coasted across the finish line at 2:15 p.m. My stats included 6 hours and 46 minutes in the saddle, with an average speed of 14.7 miles per hour.

SOUVENIRS FOR THE JOURNEY AHEAD

Having a successful outcome by completing all 100 miles strengthened me physically and mentally. Mark exemplified the qualities I'd needed to complete this epic ride: perseverance, determination, and a measure of courage. Practicing such traits was one way of honoring his memory, but I could also tap into them moving forward. Whenever I doubted myself, I could reflect on this ride to reconfirm my belief that I had the necessary strength and resilience to face other adversities.

Participating in the Tahoe event for TNT also allowed me to stand up to cancer. Mark and I had been married for nineteen years when we discovered that this disease had been silently flipping switches to hasten his mortality. One ordinary morning, we were going to the doctor to see what antibiotic Mark needed because he felt so lousy, and by that afternoon, we had a terminal diagnosis. Cancer affected both of us. For one thing, I instantly became hypervigilant and anxious about any physical malady, no matter how commonplace. Headaches meant a brain tumor, a cough suggested lung cancer, and an upset stomach was a gastrointestinal growth. Our family physician was kept busy as I brought in each of our children at the slightest pretense of ill health. Fortunately, the passage of time allowed these fears to recede slowly. In the interim, doing something that aimed at cancer gave me a sense of control, however short-term or illusory.

There were additional benefits. Joining TNT and riding with others enabled me to make friends, while the training schedule solved the problem of what to do with myself. The grander theme of funding research toward a cure imbued the project with purpose. TNT gave me the right form of structure and support to propel me forward, at least for a while.

Grieving Mark and the life I'd lost would continue to feel like the main project I was working on, but I was also beginning to realize that I needed to find something with a longer timeline. I was searching for a new role even as I was stuck in a repetitive cycle of grief that was becoming habitual, a part of how I saw myself. After all, I was the grieving widow. This dry and ugly self-pity needed to be skimmed off. But how?

CHAPTER 6
Can I gain perspective on my grief through hearing and seeing firsthand the problems of those who have no home?

TAKING AN UNEXPECTED PATH

The Community Homeless Outreach Center, CHOC for short, was located on the campus of Lancaster's Water Street Rescue Mission. The Mission's goal is to provide marginalized community members, those experiencing poverty or homelessness, with the tools they need to get back on their feet. This includes emergency shelter, meals, and basic health services. CHOC used the gym of the Mission to offer a place for the homeless to go during the day. They could escape the weather, use the restroom, bathe, hang out with others, and do laundry.

    A friend had mentioned that once a week he spent mornings helping there. Since my days were wide open and I needed ways to feel useful, I called CHOC's director, Adrian Rodriguez, to ask if they could use more volunteers. He invited me for an in-person tour. There was not much to see. The gym had ten long tables clustered in rows near the center, each with eight metal folding chairs. Well-worn magazines, a copy of the local newspaper, and a few cardboard checker sets lay strewn on top of the tables. There were about two dozen men in attendance on that day. Some sat by themselves, their heads down. Others pulled their chairs into groups, talking loudly, some over a game of cards. Most of the CHOC attendees were men, but there were also two women. They stood off to the side beneath the basketball net, their heads nodding as they conversed.

In addition to the gym, the Mission allowed CHOC to use the shower facilities and laundry in an adjacent building. Adrian said they could use a female volunteer to escort women to the showers located on a separate part of the Mission's campus, act as the attendant while they bathed, and do their laundry if requested. Was I interested?

"I can start right away," I said.

The following week, I was sitting in the windowless supply room of the shower and laundry area on an old metal chair. The decor in this area of the Mission was urban poverty minimalist. Squashed cardboard boxes on the floor contained various donations of hotel shampoo, small soaps, and other toiletries. A shelf unit along the wall sagged under the weight of clean, though ragged-looking towels. The requisite naked lightbulb dangled from a wire near the ceiling but below the exposed pipes overlaid with a thick layer of greasy dust. All this charm was contained within concrete floors and cinder block walls, both needing new paint.

The chair where I sat was around the corner from the shower stalls and sinks where the clientele washed, combed their hair, or brushed their teeth. Since they couldn't see me, they seemed to forget I was there, but *I heard everything*.

A short while earlier, I had escorted two women to the shower area. After handing them towels and toiletries, I told them to call me if they needed anything, then retreated to the supply room with a book. Their conversation clearly showed that the two had never met before.

"Ya' ever come here before?" the first woman asked.

"Nah. I hitchhiked from Virginia. Just passing through.

I wanna tell people about God." This comment was met with silence.

The Evangelist took a deep breath and said in a sharp, almost aggressive monotone, "Do you know Jesus Christ as your Lord and Savior?"

After a pause, the other woman responded with a noncommittal, "Uhhhh."

Without waiting, the Evangelist resumed, speaking so rapidly that the words were like a verbal ticker tape. "You-gotta-accept-Jesus-into-your-heart-so-he-can-cleanse-you-from-your-sin-so-you-don't-go-to-hell. Did-you-accept-Jesus? Do-you-know-God?"

A longer pause this time, and then the other woman spoke with unhurried deliberation.

"Yeah, I do, but I'm kinda pissed at him right now."

She emphasized the word "pissed." I heard a grunt, and the conversation was over. Next came the sound of the shower curtain being pulled closed and the water forcefully turning on.

When they eventually finished showering, the second woman asked the first, "Hey, ya'gotta Q-tip?" I heard rustling noises as the Evangelist dug among her bags, then apparently handed one over.

"Ahhh," said the recipient. "Thanks. Haven't had a Q-tip in a long while. I'm obliged. That feels good."

Listening to these women talk, I thought about my luxury bathroom, its cabinets filled with expensive toiletries and a stash of matching towels. I felt grateful but humbled to consider all I took for granted. Volunteering at CHOC caused me to scrutinize my daily expectations. One homeless client described the stress of never having privacy, of always worrying that his stuff would get stolen unless he was carrying it around. Others told me about fears for their physical safety, especially while sleeping, or they would casually mention the times they were knifed or got beaten up. Sure, I was grieving, but from the comfort of a lovely, shaded home in the suburbs, complete with a pool and a door lock. Hearing the conversations of the CHOC visitors gave me a new appreciation for the privacy of my refrigerator, toilet, and bedroom.

If I felt particularly depressed or grief-filled while driving to CHOC, I invariably felt lighter when I left several hours later. A typical volunteer day might include doing laundry for the homeless visitors who requested it. They were given a large trash bag to fill with their wash, and I would haul it in a rusty wagon to the laundry area. Each person's belongings required a separate load so they wouldn't get mixed up. There was just one washer and dryer, so laundry service for any given day was limited to the first four people who requested it.

I liked doing this job with the hum of the machines, the clean soap smell, and the feeling that I was doing something to improve the lives of the people who passed through the day center. I would carefully wash, dry, and fold their clothes, many of which I would have discarded as rags, smoothing out the wrinkles with my hands before sorting them by type—shirts in one pile, pants in another, socks matched and gathered into balls. I'd then put everything into a clean garbage bag and label the bag with a piece of masking tape, writing the owner's name in fancy script. If only I could clean and organize their lives as easily.

One day, I escorted a single client to the shower. Elizabeth (name changed) was new to me. Her body was like a sack of thick batter, dripping downward into folded gobs, her fullness and weight slowing her movements. Her mind, too, was slow, almost childlike, as she waited hesitantly until she was told what to do. Her clothing was stained with food, perspiration, and what appeared to be bodily fluids. The odor was staggering. Both she and the zipper on her pants were missing several teeth. A large silver safety pin strained to hold the fly closed.

Once in the shower area, I handed her towels and supplies, then returned to my chair in the supply room to give her privacy. I could hear her puffing as she shed her clothes, then the zing of metal rings on the metal rod as the shower curtain was pulled aside. Immediately, she called for me to help her. "I'll be right there," I said. When I entered, I saw that her naked skin was covered with red circular sores.

"There are fleas and roaches in my apartment," she informed me when I asked the cause. Then she said, "I can't take a shower here." She grabbed my arm, pulled me toward the stall, and pointed. A pink disposable razor rested in the soap dish attached to the wall. "I can't touch a razor. I'm on suicide watch."

Clearly, no one was watching, but perhaps just saying the words out loud offered her an emotional guardrail. I reached for the razor, then threw it out in the covered trash can a few feet away. Satisfied, Elizabeth turned on the faucet and let the water run until it was steaming hot. She was in the shower a long time. Finally, I heard the water shut off.

"Do you have any Depends?" she called from behind the curtain. "I gotta kidney problem."

"Let me check."

Returning to the supply room, I scanned the top shelves in search of adult diapers. We didn't have any, so I grabbed three large sanitary pads. I reached into the duffel I always brought to the shelter that contained my own stash of supplies. Earlier that day, I'd stopped by Walmart to purchase some packs of women's cotton panties to give out. There was a sale on Haines—six pairs for $11. I'd taken extra time to root through the inventory of mostly white to find the prettier packages containing pastels. After ripping open a package in Elizabeth's size, I held out a bouquet of panties, offering her a choice of colors. She hesitated before pointing to a light blue pair. She took them from my hand, then laid them on top of the bench next to her clothes.

"I don't wanna put these on until I get some other pants from the Mission," she said. "I wet my pants, and they stink. I been wearing them same pants and shirt for four days. I gotta meet with my parole officer tomorrow, so I gotta get some different pants."

"What did you do that you have a parole officer?" I asked.

"Arson and stabbing," she said flatly, her eyes dull.

I took a step back, my face neutral. We were alone in an isolated Mission area with thick cinder block walls that would muffle all sound. I wasn't used to thinking on my feet when presented with a challenging situation. I didn't even know if I could bluff to maintain control. She was a big woman, and I did not want to provoke her.

"You shouldn't hurt people," was all I said.

"Well, I have a temper. Sometimes, people get me real mad. But if someone here makes me mad, I'll just come and get you."

I met her eyes. "Okay. That would be a good idea."

But it was more than simply a good idea. Elizabeth realized there was an appropriate standard, that she had breached it in the past, and that she didn't want to do so again. The longing to do what was right from this simple, bruised, weary, and flea-bitten woman took my breath away. *No one is beyond hope*, I thought. Each of us carried the gift of humanity with all its potential, including the ability to care for others and try not to harm them.

Elizabeth, I cannot fix all that is wrong in your life. I can only give you an encouraging word, a steady hand to take you to the shower, to walk beside you for a very short while, to not be appalled by your smell, your sores, your flesh, or your story, to give you a pair of clean panties, to pray for you as you move forward, live, suffer, hurt inside, hurt others, disappoint, and repeat the process day after day. Maybe you are just a case to your PO, a heartache to your family, or a statistic to the local bureaucrats, but you are a lovely soul to God. Sometimes, it's hard for me to see others with His eyes.

All this went through my mind, but I could not articulate it to her. She busied herself with squeezing toothpaste onto the new toothbrush I'd given her. I recalled seeing a few men's T-shirts and pairs of scrub pants in the supply room. Perhaps I could find some for her. As I rummaged through the shelves, it occurred to me that being someone who can be present for the suffering of others was one of my strengths.

SHIFTING PERSPECTIVE TAKES TIME

I volunteered at CHOC for about a year, showing up every Friday morning for my four-hour shift. Though the shelter was less than five miles from my home, going there was like entering a different dimension, one where I was an anomaly. I was always careful to dress simply, avoiding anything that betrayed upper middle class; just having a car set me apart. During that year, I came to appreciate that though my life had a gaping wound called grief, every single one of my homeless clients would likely have changed places with me in a nanosecond.

That's what we do as humans. We compare our own situations to that of others. Usually, we look to those who have more or better. Through regular interaction with the men and women who came to CHOC, however, I was offered the perspective of contrasting my life with so many who had both less good in their lives and more bad. Theirs was not only the less relating to lack of material goods but the less resulting from a variety of factors that were positive for me but negative for them, such as circumstances of birth, parental resources, social support, education, access to healthcare, systemic racism, and available employment opportunities. They also had more of what I'd been fortunate to avoid: exposure to violence, chronic health issues, poor choices that led to encounters with law enforcement, addiction issues, and mental health problems.

Being among the homeless at CHOC helped me realize that I had strengths to offer. How could I use them? I pondered this question for several weeks.

CHAPTER 7

Can I find a framework for my life by going back to school and becoming a nurse?

THINKING WHEN YOU DON'T THINK YOU'RE THINKING

Sometimes, an idea breaks the surface, and you wonder where it originated. In what part of your soul or psyche was it composting, and for how long? Has it been on the periphery of your thinking, blurry on the edge of your visual field, but you are too busy, scared, or overwhelmed to turn your focus and gaze at it? When I look back and try to gather the scattered bits that coalesced into the decision to become a nurse, I struggle. But I remember two specific things that led up to the big commitment I made. The first was a story that inspired me. The second was telling a friend that I intended to go to nursing school.

Emerging from grief's blackest waters while carrying the weight of our family's loss had required almost two years. Only then could I take my own hard chapter and offer it as a means to help others. First, however, I just needed to get through the holidays. The Thanksgiving after Mark died, my brother and sister and their families gathered at our home as had been our custom for the previous decade. Despite the muck of grim despair that clung to me, I was the one who reluctantly sat at the head of the table, said the blessing, and carved the turkey. A few weeks later, pine-scented candles could not overcome the lingering smell of misery during Christmas. None of the kids could muster even fake enthusiasm for our traditional family outing to find a tree, so I did it alone. Even the tree itself needled me repeatedly as I wrestled it into its stand. Christmas morning was quieter without Mark's rendition of the Biblical Christmas story, our former start to the day when all five of us would knit ourselves together as we snuggled around him on the couch. I made the pancakes by myself and handed out gifts to three children who were especially kind and polite in expressing their thanks—as if good behavior could make up for what we all knew was missing. Afterward, no one danced in the kitchen.

Entering November the following year, I dreaded the holidays. I had, however, progressed to where I waited until after the kids left for school to do my morning crying. It had become as habitual as a cup of coffee to start the day. Often, my tears would stain the Bible that lay before me. God's promises to those ancient people seemed unattainable to me.

On that particular day, I read the New Testament story about an invalid who lay by the pool in Bethesda for thirty-eight long years. The pool was said to have healing waters. When Jesus passed by, he saw the man and learned how long he had suffered. "Do you want to get well?" Jesus asked him. In response, the invalid said, "I have no one to help me into the pool when the water is stirred . . ." So, Jesus immediately healed him. That's what I read. Yet what I interpreted from this was that the man was whining. He had grown accustomed to his state of brokenness, making an excuse to remain there, blaming others for not helping him.

This simple story jolted me into recognizing my own hardening complacency. I was allowing myself to remain stuck by wearing my grieving widow identity like a sash when it was time to tear it off and move on. I had challenged myself to start living more adventurously but didn't see those things as giving me a daily framework within which to function or offering a fulfilling life purpose. I asked myself the question Jesus asked the invalid. Did I want to get well? If so, I needed to shake off part of my grief stupor and find a new focus and role to fill my days.

"If you can't be decorative, be useful," was a saying Mark's mom used to indicate that most of us can't just sit around and grace others with our mere presence. So how could I be useful? Even though Mark had made sure I would never have to do so, at fifty-two, I could at least return to work. After all, my law license was still active.

I started searching for part-time positions for lawyers, but nothing sparked my interest. Doing legal research and writing briefs sounded dull, while trial work never suited my quiet, introverted personality. Eventually, I admitted that my heart wasn't in it. Nothing I'd ever done as a lawyer working on business transactions or handling real estate closings had offered deep satisfaction. It was merely a way to earn a decent living.

Although it seemed logical to use my existing degree, more thought caused me to recognize my fortunate position. Going back to the law wasn't necessary. What if I was able to use what I'd been through to create a future that would feel worthwhile?

Helping to manage Mark's end-stage disease was certainly fulfilling: administering the medications, hooking up the feeding tubes connected to his mediport, and emptying the drain bags each morning. I helped him walk, massaged his limbs, ensured he stayed warm, and found ways to enhance his comfort. By doing these tasks, I demonstrated love, showed fortitude, and transcended squeamishness. That all felt satisfying.

I certainly knew what it was like to be in a healthcare crisis. Every single person you encounter affects you when you're fighting for your life and feeling vulnerable. You become highly attuned to which individuals on the administrative and medical staff give off a gust of cold and which ones stand out because they epitomize what their role ought to be.

When Mark was sick, our lifelines were the oncology nurses who did the hands-on care. They were smart, capable, and imperturbable. Juggling the needs of several high acuity patients, administering blood products and chemotherapy, attending to beeping alarms, and communicating with other hospital team members, all while being personable and present to Mark and me, these incredible individuals were professional and compassionate. Ella Mae gave us her cell phone number so we could reach her twenty-four seven with any concerns. She made it clear that she stood beside us as Mark's advocate, working to get him every available resource within the hospital. Beth was a calming presence who bent the rules to allow a friend's daughters to play cellos and sing to Mark while he got his chemo infusion. She was also attentive to me, recognizing that I was on the cancer journey, too, and consistently offering a kind word.

An answer to what I could do floated to my mind's surface like a response to the Magic 8 Ball. Go to nursing school.

How hard could it be? I asked myself, smug in my total ignorance. After all, I had already been through law school and passed the bar exam in three states. Nursing school would be a breeze by comparison. In hindsight, my pride and arrogance were laughable.

A week or two went by. I kept my decision to myself, trying it on for a time just to make sure it felt right. Besides, I would feel obligated to follow through if I told someone. I believed I was ready, but going back to college to change careers was still a huge undertaking for anyone, let alone a single mom in her fifties.

Around this time, a friend invited me to meet for breakfast at a storefront coffee shop. The place was humming with people who had jobs to get to and busy days in front of them. We squeezed ourselves against the wall at a small table in the back near the kitchen. Waitstaff hurried past, their arms laden with plates of crispy hash browns, dippy eggs, and buttered toast.

After watching me pick at my food for a time, my friend gently reminded me that almost two years had passed since Mark's death. He and his wife knew I didn't have much to do during the day while my children attended school. Perhaps more structure could offer a reason to get out of the house and connect with people. Had I considered going back to work?

"Yes. I have," I told him. Then came the words that would reset my course for the next several years. "I'm applying to nursing school."

I had said this out loud. Telling another person sealed the deal for me.

HOW HARD CAN IT BE?

There was an excellent nursing school a few miles from my home. That afternoon, I drove to the admissions office to pick up a brochure and an application. The deadline for the incoming nursing class was six weeks away. Exiting the building, my step was light—my hands filled with papers, my heart filled with hope.

Eight weeks later, a thick envelope arrived, containing my acceptance letter for the two-year associate's degree in nursing, class of 2011. I had only applied to that one school simply because it was close enough to make the daily commute feasible. Getting in felt affirming, like opening a door to discover a welcoming smile on the other side. Reviewing the packet of materials was more sobering. Considering what was involved in returning to school took concrete form. In front of me was a detailed checklist of requirements to be completed, materials and books to purchase, and online accounts to create before matriculation.

I'd take five classes and a lab course each semester. The enormity of the task was becoming clear. I thought I could handle the academics. The question was whether I could manage being a single mom to three teenagers and overseeing everything necessary to maintain a household while attending school full time.

In terms of selecting a challenge to honor Mark's memory, this one would be all-encompassing. I realized that living fully meant more than simply doing physical adventures. It also had to include anything where I attempted to learn a new skill or, in this case, a new career. Going to nursing school would certainly meet the requirements of emulating Mark's approach to life. Though it would not be a physical adventure, changing course and reentering college in my fifties was daring. It even followed his choice of service to others through being in the medical field. I felt confident that I had made a good decision. The summer passed by quickly as I counted down the days until orientation.

Within a week of starting classes, I mentally recalculated the hours of study and the amount of perseverance, determination, and sleep deprivation required to graduate. The quantity of assigned technical reading for each class was formidable. As one instructor pointed out, I had an "old brain," so I needed extra time to memorize the gazillion things nurses must know, especially in pharmacology, anatomy, and physiology classes. Computer skills were assumed, yet like many in my generation, I was barely computer literate. When I last went to school, it was in that quaint age when teachers still wrote on blackboards. With chalk. I had a lot of catching up to do. Simultaneously, as a nursing student, I was required to immediately practice, on real humans in the hospital, the lessons from the classroom. It felt like being a brand-new driver told to merge onto a four-lane highway during rush hour—and gun it.

When I walked into my first class, sitting in the front row to better see the instructor, I was fifty-three, old enough to be a mother to most classmates and even some of my instructors. There were a handful of us nontraditional students among the 200 or so that had matriculated and one woman who was older than me, but for the most part, everyone else was right out of high school or in their early twenties. A few men were in the class, but they were the exception.

Most of my fellow nursing students were paying for college themselves, often by working as patient care assistants in the hospital or one of the nursing homes. Their determination and work ethic were impressive, motivated by a desire to better themselves and serve humanity. Nursing school involved almost none of the frivolity, partying, or socializing typically associated with the college experience.

The first weeks were a blur of assignments, meeting new people, and learning my way around the school's classrooms and labs. We were put into small groups and walked to the hospital a block away. We followed our instructor like a line of ducklings, imitating her to learn the basics of giving bed baths, doing safe patient transfers, and taking blood pressures and temperatures.

Giving a bed bath felt awkward and new. We discovered that there was a protocol to follow, that we had to think through every aspect of the process from gathering supplies to our interaction with the patient, and that we were going to do very personal care on all the body parts of a total stranger. Slowing down and being deliberate about each choice, all under the watchful eye of a tight-lipped nurse supervisor, was surprisingly taxing.

In addition to the hands-on training we received at the hospital, we were put through our paces in class. Beginning with our introductory course, foundations of nursing practice, we started to learn the critical thinking skills necessary to become effective nurses. Right out of the starting gate, the homework would keep me sitting at the kitchen table until midnight as I began to reshape myself into a nurse. Finding time to get the reading and studying done, attend class, go to clinicals, and write papers had to fit around my responsibilities as a single mom.

Even though two-plus years had passed, every morning, I still mentally refilled my pockets with recollections from the past. Mark's death and its attendant circumstances were sitting beside me all the time, competing for working memory space with whatever I was doing. Partly because of this, one aspect of medical training that surprised me was that it brought on a cascade of triggering events. For example, I now understood some of the physiological processes that had taken Mark down.

In studying disease, we learned that cancer usually begins as a single chromosomal replication mistake that goes unrepaired. If errors accumulate, this can result in cellular mutations that turn cancerous. *Aha,* I thought. Sitting in that lecture room, I realized that there was a particular day where this had happened, and I wondered which day it was. What were we doing at the exact moment when Mark's DNA went rogue? Were we together, laughing, surrounded by our three boisterous children? Were we at church, worshipping a God who already knew that certain prayers would be prayed but not answered? Was Mark performing surgery on someone else to remove their skin cancer while deep in his gut cancer was plotting its revenge?

Delving into this knowledge felt like getting to see the enemy's playbook. The brutal cunning of cancer is that it is eventually able to end-run most of the existing weapons available to fight it. As a physician, Mark knew all this. My initial hope that, somehow, he would survive his diagnosis of metastatic disease had been naive. From the start, Mark knew he was terminal.

If only we could go back, and I had Superman's ability to view things on a microscopic level, then I could have fixed this. If only his tumor had grown in a different part of his stomach rather than hiding its nasty self in the fundus, where its only symptoms were an acidic feeling that we attributed to stress. From this, my thinking went on a field trip. If only he hadn't eaten so many hot dogs as a kid, if only I hadn't cooked on a charcoal grill, if only I hadn't used Teflon pans, or if only we hadn't taken that trip to Costa Rica where he might have gotten infected with H. pylori bacteria. I deliberately attempted to redirect my thoughts because "if only" is not the vocabulary of someone who wants to move forward with attention and intention.

I knew that I was honoring Mark by pressing on in the here and now. I was able to make choices and had the opportunity to seek a fulfilling path. So many widows suffer financial devastation on top of their grief. I tended to view my situation compared to those whose husbands were still alive. No effort was required to allow self-pity and hints of enviousness to slither into my soul. But by flipping the lens, I could focus on a different truth. Having the resources and time to return to school was a privilege. I could choose to be grateful.

There was another benefit to nursing school I had not even considered. Making new friends was important to recalibrate my emotional health into positive territory. No one but a fellow nursing student could quite empathize with my screw-ups during clinical rotations. Like the time I entered a patient's room and picked up a brand new, two-pronged digital thermometer, one with a blue-based prong and one with a red-based prong. Carefully using a probe cover, I inserted the red-based prong into the patient's mouth as she lay in bed. Another nursing student, a good friend, was in the room, so I mouthed over my shoulder, "What's this blue prong for?" She looked at me with lifted brows, put her hand over her mouth, quickly turned, and left the room. I could hear muffled laughter in the hall. Later, she told me, "Red is for rectal."

That was one small mistake I never made again. Not to worry. There were so many others to fill its place. Once, I hung medicine on a patient's IV pole but forgot to close the valve on the bag, resulting in an expensive pool of liquid antibiotics on the floor. Another time, I instructed a patient to void into a little plastic cup and later received her interpretation of my words. She handed me the same container filled with a healthy quantity of stool, not the urine I expected. Or, having donned all the necessary personal protective equipment, I entered a patient's isolation room only to realize that I'd left his medicine on the cart in the hall. To exit the room, everything I wore had to be thrown out so I could start over.

Navigating the learning curve required slowing down to think, yet there was the constant pressure to speed up and cram all that needed to be accomplished into the time allotted. Some seasoned nurses were less than tolerant of shepherding nursing students, knowing that we would invariably be a drag on their schedules. They didn't see themselves as teachers and resented adding us to their list of responsibilities. Being new, we made our fair share of errors. Getting chewed out by a senior nurse was a bonding experience for our clinical group. We learned firsthand the meaning of "Nurses eat their young."

IN THEIR SHOES

Practicing compassion isn't listed on the syllabus, but it's part of the curriculum. Nurses and nursing students get to meet people at their most basic level of need. We witness births, deaths, and all manner of suffering in between.

One day, I saw an aide pushing someone in an oversized wheelchair into the patient dining room at a rehabilitation hospital. The patient, who had a stroke, was dressed in a faded cotton T-shirt and maroon sweatpants, both of which were heavily stained. Her skin had a yellowish cast, and her stringy, oil-streaked gray hair was flattened against her scalp. Since half of her body was paralyzed, she could only grimace. I took all this in while walking toward her from the checkout line, coffee in hand, my focus on the charting I needed to complete.

An hour later, I was sitting in the lounge with two other nursing students, studying for an upcoming pharmacology quiz. A charge nurse peeked around the corner and asked, "Can anyone help with a code brown?" In the hospital, colors were assigned to different emergencies. Code blue meant respiratory arrest. Code red meant fire. Code brown meant a hazardous waste spill but was often used as a slang term for fecal incontinence. All three of us jumped to volunteer. "Great. I can use all of you," she said. *All of us?* We followed her down the hall.

I entered the doorway behind the other students. Even before I fully entered the room or saw the patient, my nostrils were sucker punched by the putrid odor of human excrement. Taking a shallow breath, I looked over and recognized the woman with the stroke I'd seen earlier, now lying on her back. She was helpless, unable to muster the strength to roll over.

As a team, we stepped to her side, then worked efficiently to turn her, separate the folds of flesh, and wipe and wipe and wipe until she was finally clean. At first, I focused on the physical task while assuming a cheerful but disengaged presence as I fought against reacting to the fetid smell. As we rotated positions, however, I stood near the woman's head, holding her shoulder to keep her on her side. I forced myself to look into her eyes as they shifted across the ceiling tiles before briefly resting on my face. I glimpsed a fragment of her misery.

How would any of us feel in her position? Surely, she longed for everything everyone longs for—food, shelter, affection, happiness, attention, and love. It was not possible to watch this woman as she lay helpless in her excreta without feeling deep compassion. Being attuned to others' humanity despite the often-repulsive products of their physical bodies was never a struggle for me. I reached over to gently massage her back with my free hand while assuring her, "You're doing really well. We're almost done."

Nursing felt like a calling rather than a job. It is a responsibility and privilege to be in charge, the one standing bedside wearing gloves with medication, a needle, or a catheter in hand. Awareness of there-but-for-the-grace-of-God-go-I puts the less glamorous aspects of nursing care in proper perspective. The person on the receiving end is just like me or someone I love—a thinking, feeling, hurting human being who deserves to be treated with respect and dignity, regardless of what bodily fluids are leaking out or whatever history led to the need for care. It's also an equation that can be flipped like a coin. Disease's invasive audacity is how it can strike anyone. When Mark underwent chemo, seeing his name on the bag of cisplatin hanging from his IV pole reminded me of this fact. Hadn't he been the one performing surgery just the week before? In a single day, he went from treating others for cancer to being a cancer patient himself.

LIFE GOES ON

My first experience with a patient's death occurred in the Intensive Care Unit (ICU) a week before Christmas. The patient, PK (a pseudonym), was a woman in her forties who had cerebral palsy. PK had come to the emergency department with ongoing epileptic seizures. She did not respond to medication and descended into a coma; then she was transferred to the ICU.

My nursing care of PK involved assessing for any change in the level of consciousness, monitoring her respiratory, blood pressure, and cardiovascular status, assessing skin integrity, periodic suctioning, and positioning her to keep her airway as open as possible while minimizing the risk of increasing intracranial pressure.

One of the challenges of caring for PK was my unfamiliarity with the complex equipment in the room. Hooked to a ventilator, two separate IVs, and a telemetry monitor, PK was a small island of humanity in the middle of a tangle of plastic tubing. No prior experience had prepared me for the overwhelming technicality of the machinery it took to maintain life in the ICU.

I read the hospital's coma protocol, which included a

section on communicating with a patient who had "a prolonged decrease in consciousness." I had read *My Stroke of Insight* by Jill Bolte Taylor, a Harvard-trained brain scientist who suffered a hemorrhagic stroke at age thirty-seven and was comatose for a time. After she recovered, Dr. Taylor described in vivid detail the effects on her well-being when certain caregivers were brusque, loud, or hasty with her care.

Though PK's head injury was different, I determined that I would interact with her calmly and gently whenever I was in the room. I would hold her hand while explaining what I was about to do. I would talk to her, telling her that she was in the hospital, and it was the first week of December. When I did these things, there was no response. The only sounds were the whoosh of the ventilator and the steady beeping of the monitors to indicate the existence of barely detectable life.

We like to hear stories of Christmas miracles, but getting one is atypical. On my third clinical day working with PK, her family gathered bedside with the attending physician. After reviewing her status, they unanimously decided to discontinue ventilator support. There was no appeal, review, or waste of time. The family was directed to leave the room. Once they did so, the primary care nurse and I unhooked PK from the ventilator. We carefully washed her face and body with a warm cloth while talking to her in soothing voices. We fluffed her pillows to make her as comfortable as possible, talking to her the whole time. After we finished, the family was called back into the room. They got to say their goodbyes without the obstructing sight of a ventilator in her throat or tubing crisscrossing her body. PK died the next day.

In some hospitals, the birth of a baby is announced over the speaker system with a few soft notes of "Brahms' Lullaby." The entire hospital pauses to honor the gift of life. Death, however, is met with silence. Sometimes, the staff in attendance join to offer their final gift—a few seconds of stillness. They can do no more. Almost immediately, the wave of need presses in, draws their attention elsewhere, and they must turn to swim off. Others need saving.

Perhaps, at the end of the day, there may be time to reflect on the passing of that one life. I believe that any patient who dies leaves a mark on each person who cared for him or her. Some are more tragic, but each had a sacred spark that shimmered or had the potential to do so.

When I returned to the ICU, PK's room was already occupied by another patient. The daily rhythms of a hospital illustrate Robert Frost's observation about life: "It goes on." Becoming a nurse enabled the force of its tide to find me again.

A NURSE'S PURPOSE

Deciding to become a nurse gave me two things that had passed from my life along with my husband: structure and purpose. Going back to school with the intent of starting a different career imposed immediate structure on my days and hours. For the previous two years, creating an agenda to get through each day required significant energy, but I had almost none, depleted by a double whammy of grief and depression. The result was day after day of sitting, thinking dark thoughts, and listening to my wretched tears, which, of course, only worsened my depression. Eventually, I sought and got professional help. Yet, it was moving in a new direction that enhanced the antidepressants and grief therapy to full effect. It wasn't just that I had a way to fill my hours. I adopted a whole new identity to replace seeing myself as a widow without purpose.

When I decided to give up my law career to be home full time, I weighed my role versus my husband's in terms of how we contributed to our family and society. As a doctor specializing in skin cancer surgery, Mark's skills were in high demand, evidenced by the months-long waiting list to see him. As a business attorney, my skills were less important. Also, I never really loved my career, though I was proud of how hard I'd worked to become a lawyer and the respect it earned me.

I could choose whether to work without needing to consider the economics. This was a privilege few had. Additionally, I believed I was supporting Mark by handling the responsibilities of home and family as my full-time job. He agreed. I was fulfilled in my choice because I saw a bigger purpose than the one I'd had as a lawyer. He could be the best doctor possible because the stability I provided on the domestic front allowed him to focus better on the demands of his practice. Though he never asked or expected that I would be full time at home, he frequently voiced appreciation for the sacrifice of my choice. Divide and conquer was our motto.

When he died, I not only lost my spouse, but I lost that sense of connection to a bigger design for my life. Taking care of my family no longer served the aim of supporting my husband's medical career. Part of grieving was the despair of being cut loose from feeling useful in that way. Yes, I was still a mother, something I loved, but that wasn't enough for me as an end in itself. Plus, the job had a limited duration, the bulk of it over once I nurtured three children into adulthood. By reaching for a new career in nursing, I regained a reason to move forward.

Nursing satisfied my need to have an underlying frame for existence that includes a bigger purpose. To lead a personally fulfilling life, I need to feel that I'm contributing to a greater cause than my happiness. I want to use my time to support a value that benefits society, like healing, teaching, building, or serving others. I am motivated to "leave the world a better place."

Having decided to become a nurse, the concern about having too much time on my hands evaporated. I no longer had to wonder whether I'd find enough to do each day. Even as I negotiated morning traffic to make an 8 a.m. class, I was grateful to have a full agenda. Having a reason to get up and something to do gave me a foundation to rebuild my mental health around a new life goal. Establishing a different "why" enabled me to recruit the necessary inner resources to figure out the "how."

CHAPTER 8
Can I make a difference, and if so, how?

A NEW ADVENTURE

Once I passed my nursing boards, I began volunteering at a local homeless shelter's medical clinic. I'd only been there a few weeks when I saw an announcement for an upcoming medical mission trip to Peru. "Contact Dr. Scott if you have any questions," the notice read.

"Is there a place on the Peru trip for a newly graduated nurse with little experience?" I queried in an email.

"Yes. Absolutely," he responded.

"I have a nursing friend who has a background as a midwife. Could she come too?"

"That would be terrific," he said.

Not long thereafter, the small group going to Peru sat in Dr. Scott's living room. We listened to a woman named Anna tell her story. The impetus for this trip began with a tragedy that had occurred decades earlier.

Anna was nine years old when the school bus she was riding in tipped over. Its driver lost control coming down the treacherous mountain roads outside her hometown of Huánuco, Peru. Anna crawled out of the wreckage and heard someone scream, "That girl lost her arm!" Only when she looked down did she see the bloody stump where her forearm used to be.

Despite the crashed bus and crying children, other drivers passed by the accident scene without stopping. Finally, a farmer in a pickup truck pulled over to assist. Anna was hoisted into the truck's open bed and rushed into town. She was in agony. It felt like her left side was being dipped in acid as the cold air pressed into the exposed nerve endings of her unprotected stub.

The only available medical facility was a crumbling cinder block clinic partly staffed by practitioners with poor training. Rumors suggested that some simply bought their medical licenses from a corrupt bureaucracy. Anna almost died during her stay. The lack of appropriate medicines and medical supplies made the situation even worse. Her family, church, and neighbors brought the daily food, bedding, and clothes required since these were the patient's responsibility. When Anna needed blood, her mother called everyone she knew, and a line to donate formed outside the dilapidated walls of the so-called hospital. After three months as an inpatient, Anna was finally discharged to life in a culture where disfigurement usually results in social exclusion.

During Anna's teens, a chance meeting with an American missionary began an unlikely series of events. Ultimately, the missionary told a Florida couple about Anna, and they sponsored her to come to the United States. The goal was for her to be fitted with a prosthesis. First, however, she needed to endure several surgeries to repair her stump so the prosthesis would fit. Anna remained in the US for an extended time because of these surgeries as well as the healing required between operations. She attended English classes at a local college and met an American man named Wes. Years later, their paths would cross again when he worked in Venezuela. They would fall in love, and Anna would move to the United States to marry him. After becoming a US citizen, she vowed to one day return to Huánuco to give back to the community that saved her life.

Now in her forties, Anna met Dr. Scott because they attended the same church in Lancaster. Together, they decided to offer a free medical clinic in Huánuco. Anna shared her compelling story at the orientation meeting for this first mission trip. Until she spoke, I hadn't noticed how her one forearm never moved or the frozen position of her left fingers. A beaded bracelet rested on her wrist, just above a hand made of plastic and silicone.

ENTERING THE LAND OF THE INCAS

A few weeks later, I was on a full flight to Lima with my friend, Kendra, a fellow nurse. After clearing customs, we met our contact, an American missionary aptly named Angela. Her presence and smile provided an anchor of familiarity amid the airport hustle, the signs all in Spanish, and the exhaustion of having been awake for twenty hours. We were too tired to ask questions as Angela walked us out to a waiting car and gave the driver an address. "Someone will meet you in front of the hotel tomorrow morning at 8 a.m.," she told us. She stood on the curb and waved goodbye.

It was close to midnight when the cab driver pulled up to a seedy four-story building on the edge of the city, quickly pulled our suitcases out of the trunk, and sped away. Kendra and I looked around. The road was empty of cars, people, or movement. A single streetlight offered a bluish cast on the crumbling sidewalk in front of a set of scarred wooden doors. Was there some mistake? Not knowing what else to do, we pushed open the doors and stepped inside.

The hotel's entry room was narrow, its maize-colored walls decorated with a calendar advertising Callao beer and a tattered poster of bikini-clad women. Sitting on a stool behind a counter was a man with oily black hair wearing the red and white shirt of the Peruvian Football Federation. He was completely enclosed in a small booth with a thick plate glass window. I could hear the sounds of a game coming from the television he was watching. Barely glancing up, he gestured to a wallet-sized cutout just above the counter. We slid our passports and credit cards to him, and he, in return, slid us a metal room key on a numbered wooden stick. He didn't smile but merely took our documents and money, shoved the key out, and pointed to a stairwell on the side of the building. He made a hand motion indicating that we were dismissed.

The stairs were similar to a fire escape's, with open steel slats. We dragged our suitcases to the third floor, banging them behind us before entering a dim, bare hallway and finding our room. It took some fussing with the door lock before we eventually got the key to work. Opening the scratched metal door, we flipped on the light. A single bulb hanging from the ceiling revealed a well-worn chest of drawers and two beds—a cot with rusty springs covered by a thin, yellowed mattress and a sagging twin reminiscent of a tired, swayback horse. The floor was a speckled muddy brown linoleum, ideal for camouflaging the dust. A jagged, watermelon-sized hole in the corner of the room's cinder block wall provided ventilation to the chilly night air. A single window offered a view into an alley where, despite the late hour, we could hear a group of neighborhood kids shouting as they played. We peeked out at them. Five boys, ten to twelve years old, kicked a faded soccer ball in the tiny dirt yard between the buildings.

Kendra and I began getting ready to turn in for the night. We talked in whispers and laughed nervously to find ourselves alone in a seemingly unsafe and inhospitable place. Kendra attempted to shower. When she turned the faucet on, a small drizzle of grayish cold liquid dribbled from the pipe that jutted out from the cracked tile behind a plastic curtain. She decided to wash with the disposable wipes she'd brought.

Before climbing into bed, we dragged the room's small bureau in front of the door as a precautionary measure. We were afraid of an intruder but also of bedbugs, so we did what full-fledged adults do under such circumstances. We chose to sleep together on the single, itty-bitty cot. We could fit by laying on our sides, though it was hardly comfortable.

We lay there, silent but awake, until the continued sounds of the boys playing soccer motivated Kendra to take action. She got up, threw open the window, and yelled at them with the little Spanish she knew. "¡Alto! ¡Basta! ¡Vete!" [Stop. Enough. Go away!] Perhaps startled, the boys did as asked. Unfortunately, once the boys were gone, the street dogs took their place, barking their hunger and longing into the wee hours. Eventually, we slept anyway, exhausted from our long day of travel.

The next morning, light coming in through the dust-stained window tickled my face and woke me. As I repositioned my shoulder, my movement bumped Kendra, who opened her eyes. Our noses inches apart, we looked at each other and laughed. Our surroundings looked less frightening in daylight. I headed for the bathroom. The water heater must have kicked on during the night. I was grateful to receive a tepid shower rather than an ice-cold one. We dressed quickly, eager to leave the awful room.

A few hours later, we assembled with the rest of the mission team back in the Lima airport for our short flight over the Andes to reach the small town of Huánuco. In addition to Anna, included among the team were two doctors, Dr. Scott and Dr. Steve, a medical student graduate, Dr. Rana, a pharmacist, Gary, and nurses Grace, Angela, Melissa, Kendra, and me. We were excited to be on the cusp of what we had come here for—to provide medical services to those who otherwise would not get them. For several of us, me included, this was our first experience as a medical missionary.

Our purpose was to bring free American medical care to a rural area with limited access to health practitioners. We wanted to help the community by diagnosing problems, bringing medicines, and teaching basic sanitation practices. Providing these services to people who don't have them generally seems like a good idea. North Americans are comfortable with the soft evangelism of offering handouts to those in Third World countries. This view of how to assist was so ingrained in my thinking that I didn't even realize how ethnocentric it was or stop to consider the superiority it reflected. Through immersion, I was about to begin a crash course that enabled me to gain perspective on the potential pitfalls of short-term mission trips.

WELCOME TO HUÁNUCO

Anna had traveled ahead of us to visit her relatives in Huánuco and help with final preparations for the team's arrival. She and her sister Orpha met us at the single-runway airport on the edge of Huánuco. Ten of us climbed into two small cars and headed to Orpha's house for a welcome lunch.

We drove through narrow streets alive with pedestrians and crowded with scooters and three-wheeled moto-taxis. One block featured shops with open doors where we could see piles of fruits and boxes overflowing with vegetables. The carcasses of pigs, fowl, and cattle hung by hooks in the windows. On the sidewalk, a man was dragging a milk crate that had several pairs of chicken feet sticking out the top. A motorcycle passed us with a toddler precariously balanced on the handlebars. Regardless of the form of transport, everyone honked enthusiastically to tell everyone else to get out of the way.

Orpha lived with her two children and husband Benny, a pastor who helped to organize our medical clinic through his church. A feast was prepared for us by a local woman hired solely to cook for the missionary team during our trip. Lunch included chicken stew, rice, disinfected lettuce, olives, hard-boiled eggs, and potatoes. Anna told us that there are close to 1,000 varieties of potatoes in Peru. As we gathered around the table, I considered all the work that had gone into hosting us so we could serve the community. I would observe this repeatedly as the week went by.

After lunch, we were driven to our hostel. The owner informed us that the electricity went off at 8 p.m., and hot water was only available in the mornings—if it was available at all. We discovered that strong quad muscles are an advantage when traveling in rural Peru since toilet seats are a luxury not generally provided.

This was the first time any church in Huánuco had attempted to do something like our free medical clinic. "We will learn together. We will learn by doing," said a representative from the Presbytery of the twenty-four churches in the area who had come to welcome us. The church community had been anticipating our team's arrival for almost a year. The local church's role as a social service provider was a new concept in Peru. The church primarily saw itself as helping with spiritual teaching but was attempting to expand to encompass people's physical needs.

Invitations to the clinic had been given to the poor, and Benny's church had been working for several months to organize the event. Thought had been given and roles assigned to church volunteers to handle each of the following: organization of manpower, publicity, cleaning and supplies, facilities and room preparation, audio-visual aids, crowd control, kitchen and food preparation for the church volunteers and the mission team, pastoral help regarding spiritual needs, and interpreters/translation services for those who did not speak Spanish. In addition, several Huánuco nurses, a local eye doctor, and a local cardiologist were recruited to volunteer alongside the mission team.

Our four days of "free" medical services cost a lot in time and resources, but what yardstick can measure the intangible gains? Aside from offering care to the community, this project created the opportunity for international cooperation, relationship building, personal growth for each person involved, perspective shifts, spiritual strengthening, cultural awareness, and building mutual respect. Whether these intangibles were enough to justify the costs is a complex question worth pondering.

Our clinic took place in a church with a long name: Iglesia Evangelica Peruana Crespo Castillo Huánuco Centro. The days were long too. We opened the church's front doors at 8:30 a.m. to a line of people that stretched down the block and around the corner. Some of them had gotten up in the middle of the night to walk as far as ten miles to see an American doctor. We took patients until 2:30 p.m., had a short lunch break, then worked until 8:30 p.m. After that, we would have a meeting to try to make the following day run smoother. On average, we saw 200 patients each day. No one was turned away. We worked overtime to ensure this.

My role varied throughout the day. I might work in triage, sitting at a small wooden table in the sanctuary to take vital signs and attempt to determine the chief complaint, or in the pharmacy area where we filled the doctor's orders with the medications and vitamins we brought from the US, or alongside one of the doctors in the makeshift examination rooms in the children's dirt-floored Sunday School classrooms. The most common concerns were gastrointestinal issues, headache, worms, arthritis, hypotension from failure or inability to stay hydrated, malnutrition, eye problems, and wound infection.

One of the sadder cases I saw was a thirty-four-year-old woman who came to triage, a sleeping baby swaddled onto her back. She had a benign growth in one of her eyes that had grown to cover her entire iris, but that was not her worst problem. Through the translator, I learned that she had been hemorrhaging for a year due to uterine cancer. Her mother had died of it only recently, leaving her without family in the area. The local ophthalmologist who assisted our clinic could help with the pterygium (the benign growth) in this patient's eye, but treating her cancer was beyond what we could offer. The baby was the youngest of five children. What would become of them?

After taking down the history and sending the woman and her baby to see the doctor, I asked the translator to give me a moment before bringing in the next patient. Recognizing and accepting limitations on what can be done in the face of another's suffering is challenging for a middle-class, can-do American. In front of me was someone who lacked what I took for granted: access to primary care and needed medicines. She was also impoverished, seemingly alone, and without choice or prospects. Her cancer was probably terminal. Like grief, there was no quick fix, and this story was hard to brush away. All I could offer was what personal experience had taught me—that merely acknowledging someone else's pain or adversity can be therapeutic for the sufferer. Like many patients, this woman's situation reflected intractable, systemic problems, not anything we could address through our pop-up clinic.

Healthcare costs were a significant constraining factor for virtually everyone at the clinic. Edwin, one of the translators, explained how the local medical system worked. One "hospital" and two small medical clinics were the main sources of care. When someone could afford to see a doctor, there was still a long wait for an appointment. Doctors wanted to be paid upfront. If a patient couldn't pay, the doctor turned that person away. "They don't care," Edwin said. For every person who couldn't pay, the doctor figured there were plenty of others who could. Government health insurance existed for the poor, but there were obstacles: the individual had to travel to Lima to apply in person, the forms were complicated, and the processing time was described as exceedingly slow. The safety net was a mirage, something the government could say it offered while erecting barriers to ensure that few could access the benefits.

COMPASSION FATIGUE

When I first looked into participating in this trip, I remember being surprised that we would travel so far and yet only offer four clinic days. Midway through the third day, however, I knew why. Going on a medical mission trip is the only way to understand what it's like. The best part of me wanted to give, help, and be poured out. It's easy to believe you are capable of being virtuous from the comfort of your home in the United States. Then you travel to a Third World place, face the endless need, the countless people to serve, the dirt, the poverty, and your own physical discomfort and stress. You may realize that you're not as noble as you thought.

Sometime in the afternoon of day three, I noticed my attitude slipping. I was getting compassion weary from hearing the same symptoms repeatedly, typically indicating intestinal worms from poor sanitation. We gave out anti-worming medication, yet I knew that once these were finished, the person would likely contract worms again. Though we discussed the importance of hand washing when we provided the medicine, it was unlikely that our few minutes of instruction would affect lifelong patterns of ignoring hand washing. I wondered what we were actually accomplishing. Instead of remembering that seeing an American doctor was a special opportunity for most clinic patients, I saw only a blur of unremitting need by day's end.

I felt inadequate due to my lack of nursing experience and inability to speak Spanish, fearful regarding exposure to the patients' diseases, many due to gaps in basic sanitation, and irritable due to exhaustion, hunger, and a full bladder. I avoided tending to this last need as long as humanly possible. The church's sole toilet lacked a seat and had a rim crusted with splatters of dried urine. Despite this, the bowl was overused and overflowing. I had seen small children's bare bottoms perched on that pee-stained rim, their hands gripping its edge so they wouldn't fall. Nothing was provided to wash up afterward, and naturally, those little hands would touch everything in sight, including their food. It was no surprise gastrointestinal diseases and worms were rampant. Instead of anti-worming medications, the real need was education, clean water, and soap.

Though incapable of affecting the existing systems, on my last day, I decided to look for a way to display a caring and compassionate attitude no matter how brief the patient interaction. When I did vitals, I used my limited Spanish to attempt to make a connection. When I checked a pulse, I held the person's other hand to offer a therapeutic touch. When assigned to the pharmacy station, I smiled while handing out medications and tried to practice Spanish.

By 11 a.m., my stomach rumbled with hunger. I was sweaty and hot. Though I had access to water and a granola bar, the people I served had neither. In a small effort to feel solidarity with what they experienced daily, I pressed on, giving my drink and snack to a mother with a small child. She had been waiting in the clinic's line since 6 a.m.

HARD KNOCK LIFE

That afternoon, I went on a house call with Dr. Scott, Anna, and a church elder. The patient was a forty-year-old woman whose husband had seen the posters about an American doctor coming to Huánuco and had contacted the church. His wife was unable to leave their apartment due to a combination of physical weakness and the treacherous obstacle course between their front door and the street. This was all I knew as we left the church and set out on a brisk walk through town.

I kept my eyes on where to put my feet because of the occasional craters or buckled slabs on the sidewalk, none covered or marked. Eventually, I followed Dr. Scott and the others down a damp alleyway barely wider than our shoulders.

This led us to a dilapidated two-story structure, but to reach it required crossing a putrid, open drainage ditch several feet wide. A makeshift bridge consisting of a few two-by-fours laid side by side served that purpose. Once across, we made our way up two flights of rickety wooden stairs, then along an outdoor passageway to get to the patient's door.

Anna knocked and said, "Hello, I've brought the doctor," in Spanish.

We were greeted by a compact, middle-aged man with a deeply lined brow and thick, concrete-dusted hands. He smiled while looking at the floor and motioned for us to enter. The four of us crammed inside. The entire apartment was no bigger than a single motel room. A flimsy wall divided the cooking area from the sleeping area. Entering the bedroom, we saw a dark-haired, apple-bellied woman lying prone on a rumpled bed. Her lips were pulled into a grimace, and she moaned softly.

Dr. Scott introduced himself, then stepped over and began gently assessing her. I perched gingerly on the edge of the small stuffed chair jammed into the corner, hoping there were no bugs. Dr. Scott asked questions through an interpreter as he laid his palms on the woman's joints and probed with his fingers.

While watching the examination, I wondered about living at this poverty level and tentatively palpated the reality of its contours. Two beds made an L shape, which took up most of the floor space. Cardboard and duct tape patched the sole cracked window, which looked out onto the neighboring building. A dingy sheet hanging from the ceiling offered the only privacy between the parents and their daughter. The walls were covered with a few faded posters, some family photos, and a framed picture of the Virgin Mary. We were told that the woman in bed rarely got up. This was all the world that she could see.

Dr. Scott diagnosed her with severe brittle bone disease exacerbated by loss of muscle tone due to inactivity. He gave her several kinds of nutrition supplements, analgesics for pain, and several range of motion exercises she could do—holding cans of vegetables for weights and using balls of socks to strengthen her hands. Afterward, we had a time of extended prayer for the family and patient, each praying in our own language.

No one spoke on the walk back to the church. Individually, we retreated into a needed silence to process what we had just seen.

There is no quick or easy answer to fix problems that span multiple layers of human misery. We do not have the power or ability to hand out a few medications, snap our fingers, and make someone else's life right. Perhaps what we gave the woman in the way of visiting, listening, and praying for her ultimately accomplished something greater than whatever the vitamins and exercise program might have achieved. Like loaves and fishes, we can only offer the small bit we have, trusting that some miracle may result.

EVALUATING THE OUTCOME

That evening, after the clinic finished at 7 p.m., the Peruvian volunteers celebrated at the church to conclude our remarkable week. Despite the language and cultural differences, we had all worked together in unity of purpose and harmony of action. While in Peru, our team of two doctors, a medical student graduate, five American nurses, a pharmacist, and two facilitators saw 876 patients in four days. The significance of our trip was not necessarily that optimum health outcomes were achieved through a temporary clinic, but that 876 lives, and perhaps the lives of those who knew or loved the 876, had been touched by the kindness of our team who had journeyed so far to care for them.

I joined the mission team as a newly graduated nurse intending to be a giver. Upon my return from Peru, I felt buoyed by our team's accomplishments in providing care to indigenous people in a remote community. A few months later, after studying the long-term effects on Third World countries of some medical mission trips, I wondered whether I had taken far more than I contributed and potentially even caused harm to the existing social structures of the area. A parable from the book *When Helping Hurts* by Steve Corbett and Brian Fikkert gave me reason to reconsider the ramifications of what we had provided.

> "Let me tell you a story about Americans," an African Christian friend told [Dr. Miriam Adeney].
>
> "Elephant and Mouse were best friends. One day Elephant said, 'Mouse, let's have a party!' Animals gathered from far and near. They ate. They drank. They sang. And they danced. And nobody celebrated more and danced harder than Elephant. After the party was over, Elephant exclaimed, 'Mouse, did you ever go to a better party? What a blast!'
>
> But Mouse did not answer.
>
> 'Mouse, where are you?' Elephant called. He looked around for his friend, and then shrank back in horror. There at Elephant's feet lay Mouse. His little body was ground into the dirt. He had been smashed by the big feet of his exuberant friend, Elephant. Sometimes, that is what it is like to do missions with you Americans," the African storyteller commented. "It is like dancing with an Elephant."

I thought about all the costs of offering our four-day clinic and wondered whether we had used resources that would have been better spent in other ways. Perhaps we had merely swooped in to offer short-term solutions to chronic problems and then left. My naivete in thinking I had done a good thing when possibly I had not weighed on my mind. I rarely talked about the trip.

Ultimately, I had an opportunity to return to Peru with the same mission team two years later. Initially, I declined. When Kendra, the nurse who had also been on the first trip, asked me why, I told her about my concerns. Even if we intended to do good, had we achieved a good result?

Perspective can alter everything. We can get stuck in seeing something in a given way. An open mind and new information are necessary for gaining a different view. Kendra reminded me that there were several Peruvians whose lives were radically changed by our work.

There was the young teenager with a clubfoot for whom we had an orthopedic shoe made that allowed her to walk almost normally. She smiled shyly when she put on her new pair of shoes. There was also a man who learned from Dr. Scott that he did *not* need to have both his legs amputated as the local "expert" had opined. The only thing wrong with this patient was that he had poor peripheral circulation. His leg muscles had become weak from disuse because he had followed the advice given by a quack to stay off his feet at all times. Amputation was certainly not needed; he simply had to begin moving again. When the translator told him this, the man sobbed in relief. He was a former professional soccer player who was just forty-six years old. If nothing else, Kendra said, those two cases alone justified our trip. Yet they were house calls she had been on that I had not, so I had forgotten about them.

I also learned from the team's organizer how our kindness had made a positive difference in the region's perception of the United States. Citizens from Huánuco thanked our team's local contacts in Peru repeatedly for our visit. The community had been so moved that Americans had come to help the people that they decided they should take steps to help themselves. Healthcare initiatives had begun, and the church that sponsored our clinic had become a center of renewed interest in improving the lives of community members. I had not known this.

The power of unexpected kindnesses by relative strangers is something I do know from personal experience. When I think about those times when I was the beneficiary, there is an aura of the sacred involved, as though God personally sent an angel to offer strength at just the right time. Decades later, I still remember some of these events in my own life where a stranger appeared out of nowhere to help. Apparently, our kindness alone had a similar encouraging effect on many of the Peruvians we met. After careful consideration, I went back to Peru a second time.

I realize that nothing I did in Peru was extraordinary, and my presence was not critical. Yet I had the time, interest, and resources to participate. While it would have been wonderful to be a hero, able to bring a unique or rare skill, what I did was merely show up and do the best I could. Though I was scared of the unknowns, I took the initiative to do the trip and recruited a friend to join me. I paid my way. I worked hard. I was kind (mostly).

I learned in Peru that sometimes doing what you can has to be sufficient. I am an ordinary person, not extraordinary, but to function properly, the world needs lots of ordinary people who will do their assigned jobs, show initiative, take on new roles, and attempt to give others the love and connectedness they need. Lifting others lifts you, too.

CHAPTER 9

Do I want to be *fully alive* despite ongoing grief?

HOUSE OF BLUES

Six years had passed since Mark died. From all appearances, I had adjusted to the new normal. Yet, even as I went through the motions of moving forward, sometimes with a surface enthusiasm that fooled even me, it didn't take much for the mask to slip. A few bars of a song, the sight of an older couple holding hands, driving near Mark's old office, or a hundred other little things could remind me of how life used to be. These sounds and images would feed into a sad yearning and could trip me up for hours or even days.

Though I tried to hermetically seal my sadness, invariably, it seeped out. My husband's death was ancient history in a culture that expects loss, no matter how traumatic, to resolve itself in a year or less. People are uncomfortable with bereavement that lingers. No one was interested in hearing about mine. There was still a vast reservoir of sorrow behind the facade of normalcy, but talking about it was not encouraged. People would listen with varying degrees of politeness and then quickly change the subject. I got the message. The weight of what I'd experienced had to be carried silently.

A core problem was that I longed for a deep connection with another, yet no one was willing or able to take the position. Mark had filled the role too well. He had been the one person who understood my heart, had seen my worst flaws, still saw the best in me, and accepted me as myself. Even my parents had not done this, but with him, I had finally found my place to belong.

His unconditional support had provided me with what I needed to function well. Mark was a smart, accomplished person and a natural leader, someone whose opinions were valued and respected. To have his love and esteem validated me. When this emotional security was stolen, it was like losing the specific gravity that I'd used to balance myself in the world. Figuring a way forward would never be as easy without the ballast he had provided. Why wouldn't I continue to notice that what I'd once had . . . I didn't have anymore and would likely never have again? Was it really odd to continue grieving about that, even if six years had passed?

My previous identity as half of a certain husband and wife duo no longer existed. Like a left glove without its corresponding right, it still has its inherent value, but to what purpose? I was doing my best and had made tremendous progress in finding a different career and building a new life, but that did not erase how unloved and lonely I felt on a regular basis. When the heavy sadness washed over me, pulling me under, hopefulness seemed like some flimsy raft floating beyond reach out to sea. On the worst days, I'd wish that I had died instead of Mark, or I'd abstractly long for life to be over. I say abstractly because I did not have a plan to make this happen. These dark thoughts were just a security blanket, giving me the illusion of choice as to how to stop the pain.

Despite my melancholy tendencies, a competing and unknown force compelled me to look for distractions or escape, especially with other people. An opportunity presented itself about that time. A friend had some business to complete in Southern California and wanted to make a vacation out of it. When asked if I'd like to go, I eagerly said yes.

AND NOW FOR SOMETHING COMPLETELY DIFFERENT

The evening we arrived, we found ourselves strolling the Santa Monica Pier, a place neither of us had ever seen. There was no agenda other than to explore. We passed a cyclone fence enclosing an area the size of a high school basketball court. A small chalkboard sign announced that this was the New York Trapeze School. I stood mesmerized, watching ordinary-looking people swinging high up in the air.

When I was a kid, our family had gone to the Ringling Brothers Barnum & Bailey Circus. My younger self had been enthralled by the graceful performers doing midair somersaults and exchanging places on the trapeze. The very idea of the trapeze mixed excitement and daring with strength, athleticism, and beauty.

The trapeze students continued to practice. It looked fun. After watching for a time, I walked over to the small booth and signed myself up for an introductory class the next morning, conveniently forgetting that I was acrophobic.

I was the first to arrive for the two-hour class for novices. Eventually, six other students made their way in, all younger than me by a decade or more. We met the three instructors—Kevin, Sean, and Jordan—and got right to business. After some stretching exercises, we were each fitted with a wide canvas safety belt, which was strapped, corset-tight, around our waist. Some instructions were given about what we should do once we climbed to the platform. I was too excited to listen carefully, figuring I'd see what the other students did and follow suit. Kevin gave each of us a number. Mine was number four. Without further ado, student number one was called to begin climbing the skinny aluminum ladder.

I watched the others before me. It didn't look too difficult to scramble up to the platform, reach for and hold onto the trapeze, and swing forward with your arms over your head. The tricky part seemed to be on the backward swing. The objective was to pull your knees to your chest, then thread your legs through the space between your arms and the bar so the crook of your knees was over the bar. If you accomplished that, the next step was to let go and swing upside down by your knees alone.

None of the three students in front of me could do so. One slipped off the bar on the first swing, another's legs refused to come up, and the third student got his legs over the bar but could not bring himself to let go. Each time, Kevin gently eased the student to the safety net near the ground using the rope attached to the student's belt.

"Number four, let's go!"

As with many other things, it looks easy until you try it. Reaching up, I grabbed the ladder's side rails and began climbing. The higher I got, the more my fear of heights kicked in and the more discipline it took to keep going. Consider that a typical home step ladder has eight rungs. Add another twenty, and you get an idea of the height involved. The platform sat three stories above the pier. I forced myself up all twenty-eight rungs by sliding my palms up the rails and pulling myself skyward. When I reached the top, the ladder rails ended, and my hands had nowhere to go. The upper half of my body was adjacent to the edge of a flat surface the size of a beach towel. Sean was waiting there. I took a deep, deliberate breath and hauled myself onto the skinny perch.

I lay there on my stomach, looking and feeling like a flounder out of water, my fingers groping like a blind person's as I sought the upright bar bolted onto the platform. Using my free hand, I unclipped the carabiner end of my leash and clipped myself onto that bar. My heart was pounding and tachycardic. I gathered my legs and slowly stood up, adrenaline flooding my veins.

A tremorous "huhh-ha-hhh" sound escaped my throat as my

brain registered the dizzying feeling of standing on a tiny shelf, the ground far below in my peripheral vision. Under my breath, I repeatedly whispered the mantra, "Don't look down." Instead, I kept my chin up, looking outward on the smooth horizon of the Pacific Ocean. Seeing it calmed me, if only a small bit. On our left, a few hundred feet away, was the Santa Monica Ferris wheel, its top eye level to where we stood.

Sean took a step toward me. He unclipped my safety belt from the grab bar and clipped it onto the end of a guide rope. This rope went to an overhead pulley and then down to Kevin, who stood on the ground holding the other end. If I slipped, Kevin would catch me.

"Okay. Step over here and put your toes over the edge," Sean said. I quickly darted my eyes to the spot he indicated, two feet away from where I stood, firmly glued to the grab bar.

Seeing that I was afraid to move, he coaxed me reassuringly. "I'm right here. I have you."

I couldn't stay there forever. In a daze, I slid my feet to inch my way toward the edge, not wanting my soles to lose contact with the platform for even a moment. When I got to his side, Sean reached behind me to take hold of my back belt handle. He stood next to me, our faces as close as those of lovers, and I looked into his eyes, a handbreadth from mine. He held my gaze, the strength of his presence transmitting courage. The two of us perched there momentarily, cupped by the open sky, nothing between me and heaven except the rope on my belt and those kind, affirming eyes.

The reality of my terror was a physical weight, yet its existence caused me to recognize that I wasn't ready to die. My life felt precious. Dazed, I looked to the ocean and heard myself cry out, "I want to live!" Sean nodded and smiled, perhaps used to odd declarations from petrified students. "All right then. Lean out and get the trapeze."

He pointed to the trapeze bar dangling several feet away from the platform, held up by a hook. Reaching it required being off balance. I depended on Sean to hold the loop at the back of my belt so I wouldn't fall. Turning my shoulders to obtain the maximum extension, I stretched forward to grasp the bar with my right hand, surprised that the cold metal was so heavy. Pulling the trapeze closer, I grabbed it with my other hand. Doing this was an act of faith. I was now leaning forward over the platform's edge, with both hands in a death grip on the bar. Sean kept me from falling by counterbalancing my weight with his own, holding my belt while he leaned backward.

Throughout all these machinations, Kevin had been patiently waiting on the ground. Once he saw that I was in position, Kevin said, "When you hear 'Hep,' that's your cue to jump off."

There was no drumroll, only a moment of silence as we all stood waiting, then "Hep!" Obediently, I stepped off the platform. The next seconds were a blur.

I swung down fast, like a heavy pendulum, pulled back, and released. In a single breath, I had arched to the far end of the net. At this point, my forward motion crested, and I began to swing backward. Now Kevin yelled, "Legs up!" I was surprised to discover that the momentum of my now backward swing allowed me to bring my knees to my chest. I slid my legs over the bar and between my arms. As soon as I accomplished this, I reached the end of the backward arc and began to swing forward again. "Catch hands!" was the next command. As instructed, I let go of the bar.

If you want to know the meaning of exhilaration, try hanging by your knees while swinging upside down twenty-five feet above the ground. Even as it was happening, I was astonished. The sensation of holding onto the trapeze solely by the crook of my bent legs while the blood rushed to my head was both thrilling and empowering.

Kevin watched me complete the arc before he pulled on the guide rope attached to my harness. This plucked me off the trapeze and inverted my position. Once I was upright, he released me to fall into the safety net. My momentum caused the webbing to dip and then toss me airborne, but only a few feet. When I came down again, the net embraced me, gently swayed under my weight, and eventually eased to a full rest.

I lay on my back, staring into a cloudless sky. For a moment, all was still. Then the realization hit. *I was alive!* Facing and surviving a death-defying situation turned up the dial on all of my senses. I was aware of the simple joy of breathing. The moment was luxurious, swaddled in contentment.

This terrifying experience combined the physical sensations of falling, clutching, repositioning, and letting go. It was an exact metaphor of my grief. And in testing my limits to honor Mark, I had unexpectedly discovered my desire to truly live. Standing on the platform's edge and fearing for my life made me realize how much I wanted to keep it. I had confronted my dread of heights, recognized the strength of my survival instinct, and through that discovery found hope.

Hanging thirty feet in the air, it was as though Mark whispered into my ear, *Live your life for both of us.*

I promised him I would.

Dr. Mark H. Hassel- a dermatological surgeon, father, husband, and athlete who lived fully throughout each of his 47 years. He was courageous, smart, funny, and kind and is deeply missed.

Mark with our children, Summer 2001.

Mark and me, 2002.

Shortly after Mark began chemotherapy and his hair started falling out, he decided to go baldilocks. In solidarity with Mark, my brother David (on left) shaved his head too.

Me on stage at the Tri-Fitness competition,
Las Vegas, Nevada, 2008.

Testing my fear of heights at the New York School of Trapeze, 2013, Santa Monica, California.

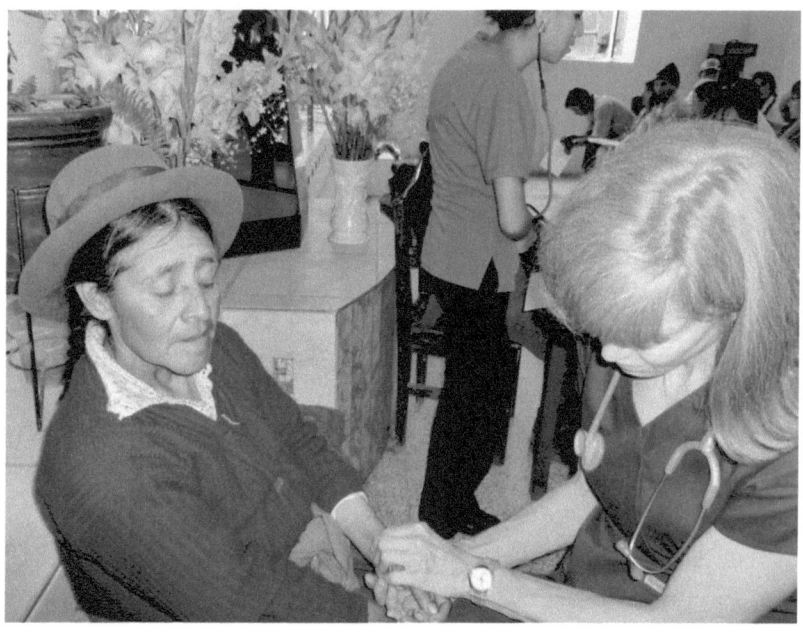

Doing a basic nursing assessment while on a medical mission trip to Huánuco, Peru, 2013.

Sitka, Alaska, 2016. This photo shows the front of my kayak in the foreground. We were close enough to the whale that I felt spray in my face when it flipped its tail flukes.

CHAPTER 10
Can I find my voice to tell my story?

A COMMON FEAR

Speaking in front of other people is a fear so common it even has a name: glossophobia. Comedian Jerry Seinfeld reportedly said, "According to most studies, people's number one fear is public speaking. Number two is death. Death is number two."

And yet, a confident speaker is a leader. There is social power and status in using your voice to direct other people's thoughts and opinions, to convince them to see a slice of the world through your eyes. I understand that public speaking is a valuable skill to have. I admire people who do this. I have never been one of them.

As a child, I was called bashful. I'd hide behind my mother's skirts and peek out warily when meeting anyone new. My shyness was an asset in a family where the rule was, "Children are to be seen and not heard." The only opinion that mattered was our father's. If we dared to speak up and disagree, we were verbally decimated. We knew nothing. Remaining quiet avoided the buzzsaw of paternal criticism. Naturally, I internalized this doubt in my views and ability to express them. I wasn't someone who lost my voice somewhere along the way. I often struggled to find it in the first place.

My go-to coping mechanism for this deficiency is to ask questions so others do the talking. I learned this in grade school.

When my dad needed to drive hours to deliver a sailboat, I was invited to tag along. Typically, I didn't spend much time with him. He wasn't fond of children and arranged his daily schedule to suit his preferences. He was still asleep in the morning when we left for school, then came home just before we went to bed. Being alone in a car with my dad made me anxious.

Having silently observed him for nine years, I knew he liked to be the one talking. He was smart and seemed to enjoy sharing his knowledge with others. Before getting in the car that day, I devised a plan. All I needed to do was think up a good question. If I asked him to explain something complicated, the focus wouldn't be on me.

"Daddy, how does a car engine work?" I asked as we pulled away from the curb.

I didn't care to know, but he didn't notice whether I was paying attention. He started to answer, and for the next half hour, I could relax, hide, and dream up my next question. Neither of us considered that I might have something interesting to contribute.

As an adult, I often revert to the same strategy I used with my dad. Speaking one-to-one with certain types of strangers, especially those I want to impress, especially if they are male, can invoke that expanding, balloon-in-my-chest feeling. When it's my turn to talk, I try to examine each thought before saying it, but, like Lucy and Ethel on the conveyor belt, I can't process the words fast enough. I become a verbal klutz, grabbing at snippets of sentences and shoving them out. Simultaneously, another part of me sits in the control room watching the disaster unfold, hyper-attuned to the other person's eyes, stealing glances at a phone or around the room.

It's so much easier to give others the spotlight. "What's keeping you busy right now?" I'll ask. Or "Have you done anything out of the ordinary lately?" This way, I can remain silent to understand that person and what interests them.

I knew it was a personal weakness to avoid being the one speaking so I could avoid judging myself for not doing it well. Perhaps I never would have addressed this deficiency except for pushing myself to "live fully," which meant committing to doing things that were an uncomfortable stretch and forced me to grow.

After trapeze school and several physical adventures completed in Mark's memory, I wondered what my next challenge could be. At the time, I was working as a nurse in the blood donor center of our local hospital. A notice in the hospital's employee newsletter asked, "Are you interested in learning public speaking and leadership skills?" An invitation to attend an informational meeting of Toastmasters was attached. I cut out the notice and slid it into the pocket of my scrubs. *What about this?*

WHAT'S A TOASTMASTER?

Toastmasters is an international, nonprofit educational organization dedicated to promoting public speaking, communication, and leadership skills. There are local clubs worldwide. Members pay dues, meet monthly, and progress through a series of workbooks by preparing and giving speeches. The speaking projects start small, then add skills step by step. Each person sets his or her pace to complete the workbook assignments. The meetings are self-run, so everyone has the chance to practice leadership by filling the various meeting roles.

I considered whether joining Toastmasters and giving speeches would be an appropriate challenge. Though not physically risky, it would push me to face a big fear. The opportunity to acquire a useful skill was involved. Add to that my memory of Mark's learned confidence as a speaker at national medical conferences. "You just need to prepare and be willing to practice" were two of his tips for success. I knew I could do it. The question was whether I would let inertia and fear of embarrassment hold me back. Again, I thought of the rocking chair test. I also wondered if my story might encourage others. Whenever I shared why I decided to go to nursing school, others reacted that I'd done something inspirational. Learning to tell this narrative to an audience might empower people to test their own limits.

Showing up for a Toastmasters meeting was my first step. After working a full nursing shift, it would have been easy to head toward the hospital parking lot instead of the corridor leading to a room full of strangers. Deliberately, I steered myself toward that meeting, where part of me did not want to go. A few minutes later, I was shaking hands with a Toastmaster.

In my imagination, I envisioned a packed auditorium of fifty people, mostly men in suits, who looked unapproachable and all knew each other. Reality was so much kinder. Scanning the room, I counted seven women and two men. Everyone smiled.

The meeting started promptly and lasted exactly sixty minutes. I was introduced as a guest, so I had to stand, state my name, and describe where I worked in the hospital. Not so hard. When I sat down, everyone clapped. There was a lot of clapping during the meeting. Each time anyone spoke, everyone clapped.

Someone gave a short teaching segment, and then one of the attendees gave a five-minute speech on the history of lobster fishing. We ended the meeting with something called "table topics"—impromptu speeches lasting one to two minutes. Typically, the speaker draws a question out of a hat, is given a moment to gather his or her thoughts, and improvises an answer on the spot.

The hour went quickly, adhering to the written agenda I'd been handed when I walked in. My impression of this group was positive, not because they were polished speakers I could study, but because they weren't. I could learn along with them, confident that this was a friendly and encouraging group where I'd feel comfortable. Each person wanted to improve, as evidenced by how he or she responded to others' suggestions. No one appeared to see themselves as above critique. We could practice together.

After the evening, I signed up, paid my dues, and received my first Pathways workbook, "Mastering Fundamentals." Later, paging through the workbook, I concluded that the program looked doable. The Toastmasters folks clearly understood the general fear associated with public speaking. The book offered practical guidelines to tamp down anxiety while stressing the importance of preparation and practice. As someone who likes written parameters and checking things off lists, I had the bumpers in place so I could begin. When I felt ready, my first speech project was "the icebreaker."

START WITH YOURSELF

An icebreaker speech is a three- to five-minute talk on a topic familiar to everyone. Themselves. This is typically the first speech a baby Toastmaster gives to an audience, and it allows the other members to get to know the person speaking. Talking about oneself should be the easiest task. No matter how blank your mind is, you can say a few words about your life.

Before writing my icebreaker, I did some research on the topic of stage fright. It was reassuring to learn that even professional, well-known performers have problems with nerves and anxiety. John Lennon was known to have vomited before most live performances. Barbra Streisand once forgot her song's lyrics during a concert in Central Park and, for twenty-seven years thereafter, refused to perform in front of an audience. Business leaders are also not immune. Warren Buffet avoided college courses that required students to speak in class. He was terrified of standing up just to say his name. When he graduated and began working as a stockbroker, he realized that his fear would hold him back unless he faced it head-on, so he took a Dale Carnegie class on public speaking. Mahatma Gandhi's career is an example of how someone with extreme social anxiety can be motivated to overcome fear. He found his courage to speak out because of a passionate belief in something bigger—the necessity of a free India. My own goals were more parochial but personally compelling, nonetheless. I simply wanted to honor my husband's memory by doing brave things.

The workbook laid out the parameters of the icebreaker speech. This was a helpful outline of how to go about the process. I studied the suggestions and got to work. I learned that the speech is not intended to merely summarize where you were born, went to school, your job, or other biographical details. Instead, the instructions suggest you focus on one story about a single aspect of your life. I decided to share why I became a nurse because that theme led me to Toastmasters. Mine was a tale of what I did after what had happened. It was about getting back up after life had smacked me down.

But how to say it in front of others and not get all teary? Though seven years had passed since Mark died, my grief was like a soldered-on locket. Usually, it was invisible under the layers I wore, but I knew it was there, always sitting just over my heart. Whenever I thought about what had happened to him and us, it opened a gateway to sadness. Among the images I could not forget was the one of my hero, post-chemo, sitting on the tile floor in our shower. He didn't hear me enter the bathroom, partly because the water was streaming over him but also because his head was between his knees while he sobbed. Knowing he would not want to be seen like that, not even by me, I backed out of the room. But I could never back out of the memory.

The man I loved had suffered horribly on every level of

existence. He did so with steadfast bravery that invariably caused me to inhale sharply and hold my breath merely to consider it. At the time, half of my agony was that my eyes were taped open to every single aspect of his suffering while being helpless to relieve it or turn away. There was the physical torture of the cancer pain itself, plus all the side effects of the toxic chemicals taken to attempt to fight it: the burning mouth ulcers and blisters, the electric needle stabbing tingles that attacked his fingers and toes, a brain fog that left him witless yet aware of his former ability, and full body soreness and achy malaise. As if these were insufficient torments, he knew that his life was slipping away and felt responsible for and powerless to stop how his disease crushed the people he loved the most.

We were impotent to change, fix, or alleviate any of this, so our miseries over these circumstances reverberated silently between us. We attempted to protect each other through our tacit pact not to discuss how much it hurt to witness each other's anguish. This went on for nineteen months, progressing in intensity until we were both exhausted with the effort it took for him to live. Finally, that last week, our pastor came to our home, met with Mark, and told him it was okay to stop. Afterward, with tears and snot streaming down our faces, the three of us held hands and prayed that God would take him quickly. Two days later, He did.

Upon reflection, the story I held in my heart felt monumental. Yet, for my first speech, I needed to take all of it and carve out a bite-sized piece about returning to school to become a nurse. It was one chapter in the bigger tale of how my desire to honor Mark's memory had the unintended fringe benefit of plugging me back into life. Becoming a nurse was just one example of remembering Mark while simultaneously finding another way to fight forward. That was the theme I needed to focus on for the icebreaker speech.

JUST FIVE MINUTES

As someone who speaks slower, I would get to say about 650 words in the five minutes allotted for an icebreaker. My job was to accomplish three things during that time: say what I needed to say succinctly, stare down stage fright, and maintain composure while relating an emotionally heavy narrative. Easy peasy, right?

Of course, it wasn't. Just writing, rewriting, and re-rewriting the speech took weeks and a concerted effort. Then, I had to force myself to practice saying it out loud. I felt shy, aware that I could be a harsh judge. The monotone sound of my voice made me cringe. I tried listening to how actors spoke on TV to imitate their voice modulation, but when I focused on that, I lost my train of thought. To better learn my lines, I repeated my speech over and over until it stuck. I whispered it to myself while driving to work or doing dishes. As a backup, I wrote the main points on index cards. I carried them around until they became crumpled and stained.

Next was practicing the speech in front of a mirror. Horrors. Watching, detached, I became my own critic. "Stand up straight, look them in the eye, stop mumbling, relax—you look tense, you're wearing *that*?" The only encouraging thing I could acknowledge was that I kept practicing. Though I didn't enjoy it and didn't want to do it, fear of flopping on stage motivated me.

My speech debut was on a Wednesday night. I wore a simple wrap dress with elegant black patent leather high heels. The choice of footwear was a crucial detail that offered me the magical *Cinderella* effect. In the right pair of shoes, a confident and graceful woman suddenly steps forward, knowing she is ready to attend the ball and capable of holding others' attention. My healthy shoe collection reflects my faith in this truth.

I arrived early, allowing ample time to make multiple trips to the loo beforehand, but I couldn't eliminate the butterflies.

After the third visit, I tried a different tactic. Fortunately, I was alone. Taking two deep breaths, I did a few power poses. First, I stood with arms stretched wide, then stood straight with my feet slightly apart, placing my fists akimbo on my hips, *Wonder Woman* style. Checking the clock, I gave my reflection a thumbs-up over the sink. *Let's roll.*

Upon entering the room, I quickly counted ten other souls in attendance. Having been to Toastmasters for several months by this point, these were people I knew. Yes, I was still nervous, but the dinner party size of the audience was reassuring. The meeting started. Halfway through the agenda, I was called forward. Now or never.

I didn't trip on the walk to the front. I got to the middle of the stage area, paused, and turned to face everyone. In Toastmasters, there is no lectern between you and the audience, so there's nowhere to hide. I took a breath, briefly blinked, and smiled. When I opened my mouth, words actually came out. I think I may have glanced at my notes a time or two. Though I remained planted in the same place the entire time and only used limited hand gestures, my voice didn't shake, I didn't forget my lines, and I spoke for the requisite five minutes. When I finished, I heard applause.

Returning to the safety of my seat was a relief. But it was more than that. There was a feeling of accomplishment, which was its own reward. The speech had gone better than I thought. The smiles and murmurs of affirmations from the audience told me they were for me and with me. Not just because we were Toastmasters together, but because of my actual message. This was like sprinkles on my cupcake. Pure joy.

I recognized that if I could do this once, I could do it again and learn to do it better. This is one of the tools of self-validation, seeing your own inner potential for achievement and improvement. Whether I chose to invest time into getting better at giving speeches, this first experience gave me the confidence to realize that, yes, it could be done. That was good enough for a start.

As it turned out, my Toastmasters pursuits lasted only a year. After that, a schedule change in my job made it impossible to attend the meetings. During that year, however, I gave three speeches and volunteered to do a few impromptu Table Topics talks. I met lovely people, had fun, and learned to stand taller inside. Though I didn't eliminate my fear of speaking in front of others, I conquered my dread of that fear. By walking through the door of a Toastmasters meeting, making the effort, and giving an icebreaker speech, I learned that I could stand up in front of strangers and say words without fainting, freezing, or losing continence. Whether I ever choose to build on that is up to me.

CHAPTER 11
Is another man necessary to fill the hole left by my husband's death?

CHASIN' YOU

I lack a psychology degree, but I have a theory about women based on personal observation. Those who had a loving relationship with their father don't seem to hunger for a man in their lives with the same desperate intensity as those of us who had careless, absent, or hurtful fathers. As small girls, we could not do much to change the dynamic of our father's hearts toward us. In adulthood, some of us try to make up for that void by heedlessly casting male partners, boyfriends, or husbands into the starring role our fathers were supposed to fill—as if that could edit our childhood so we could be read as stronger and more coherent.

Acknowledging how this theory has affected my life makes me cringe. I think learning to have self-compassion is still a wrestling match between two mindsets. Unfortunately, for me, the voice of *You ought to be perfect* is much louder than that of *You're only human*.

From the time I was a teenager, having a man felt like a necessity. I didn't connect my father's indifference to my craving to be desirable in other male eyes. I also failed to realize how men became an emotional Band-Aid after my mom suffered a fatal heart attack the week before my high school graduation. If not in a relationship, I was actively seeking one. My choices weren't horrible. I just wanted several things only a man could provide, primarily the male affirmation I'd never had. When I met Mark, I considered myself incredibly lucky. He provided the steadying hand that made me feel more confident and the love that brought me happiness.

Over the next nineteen years, we built a marriage based on reciprocal caring and mutual respect. We agreed on fundamental issues regarding money, sex, and how to raise a family. We rarely argued. When Mark wasn't working, we went biking, skiing, or hiking together. Neither of us had time-consuming individual hobbies. Early in our marriage, when I lamented that our move for his medical training meant I wouldn't make law partner, he assured me that I was his partner. He meant it.

Ultimately, we each got to thrive. His encouragement and financial success allowed me to do what I felt mattered most: nurturing our family. In return, because I handled every aspect of our domestic life, he could more fully devote himself to medicine and his practice.

For me, the frustrating part of our marriage was that there wasn't enough Mark to go around. One of the downsides of being married to someone you admire is that the things that make him exceptional are the same things that mean he has less time to spend with you. The months-long waiting list for an appointment at Mark's practice verified that he was very good at what he did. This necessitated lots of overtime. He swam most mornings before office hours and had an attractive physique to show for it. When he wasn't working, his attentiveness as a father was the highest priority. Sometimes, I'd actually complain about this. He often replied, "We'll have more time down the road. I feel this pressing urgency that my time with them is short."

I thought about these statements a lot after Mark received his terminal diagnosis. My imagined future, where I would get more one-on-one time with him, would never happen. A small bitterness became the pea under my mattress. I had staked my life on what I believed were reasonable expectations for how the years should unfold. Standing by Mark's casket at age forty-nine, stunned that I'd won the wrong lottery, was not what I envisioned.

Our bedroom became one of the venues where God and I had it out night after night. I cried, and He seemingly turned His back. Abandoned to sort it out solo, I projected my questions onto the ceiling. *What truth or love beneath that truth will enable me to survive? Did you take him because he held too high a place, there on the throne of my heart where no mortal is supposed to sit? Can you love someone too much?*

The ocean of my new reality was too frightening to navigate alone. Even as a new widow, I reverted to my pre-Mark pattern without thinking about it. I needed a man.

WHAT'S LOVE GOT TO DO WITH IT?

Judging those who are grieving is an easy sport. "Dating so soon?" People usually don't intend to be unkind. They simply don't realize that someone grieving can present the mirage of normalcy, but normalcy is an illusion. I did what I did to get through each day, not because it was appropriate. Those who judged me became people I avoided.

In the initial years following Mark's death, I was rarely without a boyfriend. The first ones didn't last longer than a few months, a year at most. They were just filler, absorbent material that could sop up some tears, but they were as discardable as a wet paper towel. I now understand that certain confusing, hurtful, or foolish behaviors are motivated by pain.

When I met Ace, I'd been widowed for five years. We seemed compatible in almost every way. He was more substantial: someone I could respect. I thought I was in love with him and even had visions of getting remarried. I let him know early on that this was what I wanted. Ace, however, could never fully commit, though whenever I brought up the subject of his intent, he always assured me that "we were moving in that direction."

After five years went by, I realized that Ace and I may have been "moving in that direction," but like an asymptote, we would never actually arrive. When I told him we were done, he didn't argue, letting me go without resistance.

Because I was angry with Ace for dangling promises but never fully committing, I immediately got on dating sites. I'd show him that he'd made a huge mistake. Besides, scanning the photos of all those who professed to be looking for love, or their model of it, was a fun diversion. I typed a message to a man, I'll call him Moose, who had a doctorate, blue eyes, and a terrific smile. His profile said that he enjoyed the outdoors, biking, and skiing, all traits that appealed to me. We sent several emails back and forth before deciding to have coffee.

When we met, I was skeptical, but not skeptical enough. It took many months for me to understand what some members of my family knew the first time they were introduced to Moose. They were just hesitant to tell me, figuring I'd eventually get there.

OOPS . . . I DID IT AGAIN!

At first, I was attracted to Moose because of all the ways he was unlike Ace. In this new relationship, I didn't have to guess what Moose was thinking or feeling or whether he was upset with me. There were no rabbit trails of misunderstanding that circled round and round the forest but eventually got nowhere. Also, I had no hopes or expectations for a long-term connection with Moose. For the first six months, I was simply delighted to have someone who thought I was special and didn't hesitate to tell me so. When Moose and I spent time together, the dynamic was easy and comfortable. He found little ways to be romantic, like slipping a wildflower on my bike seat if we stopped to get water or leaving chocolate kisses in places he knew I'd find them.

My reservations surfaced that summer. I had a few concerns earlier but chose to put them in the "nobody's perfect" column. What were they? Nothing terrible, just observations that made him a questionable partner for me. For instance, I noticed that he was always seriously at odds with at least one member of his family, usually one of his adult children or their spouses. He also seemed to have a history of misunderstandings with coworkers. Most disconcerting, however, was that he believed he was self-sufficient but was unaware of how frequently he leaned on others' resources and energy.

He often showed up at my house and, even before taking off his coat, asked if I could make him food. "You don't need to fuss. Just something simple." Other times, I would open the door to welcome him, and he'd thrust a bulging plastic bag in my direction. "Can I put this in your recycling bin?" He prided himself on his thriftiness in refusing to pay for recycling service for his household of one. Most frustrating was that he didn't have WI-FI or a printer, so he frequently wanted me to print out documents or emails he needed. Individually, these were all small asks, but strung together, these incidents indicated a troubling pattern. What was it? Obliviousness? Cheapness? I pushed down these impressions because he was sweet and thoughtful in other ways. Yet, my radar was turned on. What would it find?

LET'S PLAY GO FISH

The idea of salmon fishing in Alaska was presented by his two friends, Jim and Deb. They were planning a return trip to a tiny, remote fishing mecca on Prince of Wales Island off the coast of British Columbia that fall. Would we like to join them? They showed us photos and described the quiet wilderness, the freshwater streams where they cast for pink and silver salmon, and their dawn hikes up the Sunnahae Trail. Moose was thrilled when I said I was interested despite my lack of knowledge or background in fishing.

This was an exciting opportunity to try a new adventure. I had been to Alaska years before on a bike tour with Mark. I remembered the overhanging wild fierceness of the place. Our days alternated between beautifully crisp and misty forlorn, but it always felt as if there was an open lid to the heavens. In Alaska, there seemed to be less static between God and humanity. Returning there had always been my intent. The bonus was getting to try an activity that Moose loved.

Once we committed, Jim recommended we book a place to stay as soon as possible. The options in Craig, Alaska, population 1,036, were limited. Since Moose's requirements for shelter were less fussy than mine, we decided that I should look into finding accommodations. While I was at it, I laid out a preliminary itinerary for what Moose and I had decided would be a week-and-a-half trip.

Getting to Alaska from Philadelphia takes nineteen hours. Having traveled so far, we wanted to visit Sitka and Ketchikan and book a passage on the Alaska Marine Highway. Figuring out all the logistics took hours. Moose's lack of WI-FI access meant that the work defaulted to me. There were tickets to buy, lodgings to find, car rentals to arrange, and all the other details of our travel. Some people enjoy planning trips. I'm not one of them. Irritation that we were not sharing the burden of organizing the trip began to fester.

For his part, Moose made a list of the gear and fishing equipment I'd need to purchase. He suggested we go to an outdoor sporting goods store called Cabela's, one of his favorite places. We live an hour from one of the largest Cabela's in the United States. It's an impressive place for the sort of place it is. The showroom is over 250,000 square feet.

Entering the store, you immediately see a flock of geese hanging overhead, forever held in place by an invisible wire.

Wildlife and fish mounts are everywhere. Most notable is "Conservation Mountain," a thirty-foot-tall structure with two waterfalls and a stunning array of taxidermy, including bears, elk, moose, caribou, and mountain lions. In the African Diorama, you'll find an elephant, a rhino, lions, zebras, and hyenas, all trophies of someone who had the thrill of hunting down a wild creature in its natural habitat, shooting it, and hauling it back to the suburbs. Seeing that many stuffed and mounted animals, fish, and reptiles was astounding.

I had an idea of the outrageous expense of taxidermy since Moose's living room contained multiple specimens of his own. I thought of all the guns, energy, and resources Cabela's used to create the display in front of me. Ironically, an air-conditioned mega store was promoting the concept of a wilderness experience by pushing its extensive inventory of modern-day comforts, clothing, and equipment. There is an obvious paradox, but getting others to enjoy the outdoors is, at heart, a money business just like any other.

I had noticed early on in our relationship that Moose was a Cabela's junkie. His home was a testament to his loyalty. He served meals on Cabela's pine-cone dishes with matching mugs, relaxed on a Cabela's mountain wood sofa in his living room, and slept under a Cabela's quilt adorned with moose—the source of the nickname I'd given him. Initially, I found it amusing. Now, here we were, in the proverbial Land of Oz. He was delighted to show me around, not noticing my restrained reaction. I began to feel like the parent in me was being dragged around the store by the little boy in him.

In my family, we were not slavish loyalists to anything, not traditions or alma maters or sports teams, and certainly not brands. Moose's devotion to Cabela's seemed to reflect a dogmatic single-mindedness that was at least questionably distasteful to me. Yet these suspicions occurred below the surface. At the time, all I felt was a discomfort I couldn't pinpoint.

Mostly, I enjoyed Moose's company, and he had no glaring character flaws. Yet the more I got to know him, the more I saw how his interests and areas of strength didn't mesh well with mine. I liked doing fun activities with him, but when it came to the practicalities of daily life, there was an imbalance. He tended to be the helped rather than the helper in areas where it mattered to me. These observations dampened my enthusiasm but hadn't yet risen to the level of deal-breaker. I was willing to see how the relationship played out. Apparently, he didn't recognize that I saw the Alaska trip as a final litmus test. He thought that being together for ten days would cement our relationship. I thought traveling with him for that length of time would more likely highlight the cracks.

RIDE INTO THE DANGER ZONE

Our short flight from Ketchikan to Prince of Wales Island was a nightmare. We walked across the tarmac in misty rain to board a single-engine Cessna 206 Stationair. The aircraft could hold three passengers, but it was just Moose and me. The pilot stood by the plane's door, waiting. He was bearded, dressed in rumpled jeans and a down jacket, and, after a too-brief smile, all business. Grabbing our duffel bags, he stowed them behind the seats and directed us to climb into the plane. We did. He quickly got in behind us, moved to the cockpit, and told us to buckle up. That was the last thing he said for the next half hour. He was too busy making sure we all didn't die.

The flight seemed designed to test our faith. Within minutes of takeoff, we flew into thick clouds that reduced visibility to zero. Rain spattered the windows. The engine roared at over a hundred decibels, a constant reassurance that it was still working, but the noise made talking impossible. I looked at Moose. He tried to reassure me with his eyes, but I didn't feel reassured. The aircraft twitched and bucked like a spirit demon, with an occasional terrifying drop in altitude thrown in. I leaned forward, every muscle tense, while I stared at the pilot's back and telepathically willed him to keep us alive. *Help us, help us, help us,* I pleaded to God while holding in my scream. To distract myself, I dragged a small journal from my purse and scribbled the names of people I wanted to tell either that I loved them or that I was sorry. Someone might find it among the wreckage and realize I meant well at heart despite the particulars.

After twenty-five hair-raising minutes, we dropped below the clouds, allowing us a quick view of Klawock Harbor, Sea Otter Sound, and the dense forests of Prince of Wales Island. Following a bumpy landing, the pilot taxied toward a metal-roofed shed the size of a two-car garage. It was the airport terminal. He eased the plane to a stop. I exhaled, exhausted. All my prayer efforts had worked.

My legs shook as the pilot lifted his hand to help me out of the Cessna. Moose jumped down beside me. "That was a bit rough," he said, then turned to get our gear. Fortunately, I could see Jim and Deb standing not far away on the tarmac. The smile of a friend offers a feeling of kinship and safety, something I needed after the stressful flight.

"You made it!" Jim grinned when we walked over. He slapped Moose on the back, grabbed my duffel, and led us to the SUV he'd rented. Deb and I hung back behind the men, exchanging notes on our travel experiences. They had arrived two days earlier, and their flight was smooth and uneventful. She described the one-room cabin where they were staying, not far from the airport, rolling her eyes while calling it glorified camping, but without the glorified part.

Jim and Deb arranged dinner at Fireweed Lodge, a family-owned fishing resort outside Craig on the Klawock Estuary. We pulled up to a rambling, log-cabin-style building decorated with wooden fish and hanging pots overflowing with viola, shooting stars, and columbine. Stepping inside, we passed through a short hallway before entering the main dining area.

It was a mountain man's paradise where wood pine paneling covered every square inch of the place. A ten-foot-tall totem pole stood sentry beside a cozy stone fireplace over which a bear skin was tacked at an angle. The glassy-eyed head, with its open snarling mouth, jutted out incongruously from what was left of its deflated body. Never again would it stand on the riverbanks to haul in the sort of fish gutted and stuffed to decorate the lodge's walls.

Despite all the clutter, what saved the room from being tacky was that the entire back wall was made of glass. Two-story windows allowed a panoramic view of what we had come for: pristine water, forests, mountains, and endless sky. This lodge was a man-made fort, partly reflecting our species' triumph over claw, fang, fin, and the Alaskan weather.

We were directed to our table, where binoculars had been thoughtfully placed on the window ledge. Tall golden drafts of Alaskan Amber were set before each of us. Watching bald eagles gracefully float over the river allowed me to forget feeling like our plane would crash. We chatted excitedly about our strategy for the next day as we dove into plates of freshly caught local salmon served with roasted vegetables and warm, crusty bread. Moose was eager to start fishing, so he and Jim agreed to meet at 6 a.m. the following morning. Deb would drop them off at the creek, and then she and I could get coffee and hike. We planned to join the guys at lunchtime; then we would all fish.

THE NATURE OF THINGS

The first afternoon, Jim took Deb and me to a remote spot he'd found on his previous trip. Moose bailed on us at the last minute. He had already caught four huge coho that morning in the water closer to Craig. Rather than fishing with me in an unknown stream, he preferred to stay put. Though disappointed, I knew fishing was important to him, so I shrugged and said okay.

Moose's decision not only left Jim solely responsible for helping me fish, but it also indicated Moose's priorities. Jim good-naturedly agreed to the arrangement. We left Moose standing thigh-deep in the Klawock River while Jim, Deb, and I got into the SUV and headed north on the only road leaving town.

When I agreed to this adventure, the image in my mind was like the poster for *A River Runs Through It,* a blue sky pressed against sunlit trees beside placid waters. The reality was daily rain and mud, carrying your gear long distances through thorny underbrush, and fording treacherous streams while navigating the ferocious current.

We hiked an hour through the woods and wet mist to reach the fishing spot Jim had in mind. Nearing the water, I reached out to push aside a heavy spruce branch. With the branch still in my hand, I looked down. My boot had just missed stepping into a half-eaten fish carcass, its flesh torn apart by something hungry. I jumped back, panicked by the primal sight of the empty eye sockets, and hurried to catch up with Deb. The scent of rotting fish grew stronger as we proceeded along the bank. In the creek's backwaters, a dozen decaying salmon floated belly-up while the bodies of others had been hauled ashore to be gorged upon. Up close, the sights and smells of the circle of life had an unexpected ick factor.

Jim found a place to enter the rushing water and began wading to the other side. Deb and I followed, or at least we tried to. The creek was just above our knees in most places, but the current's force made crossing it challenging. Navigating to the far bank was like trying to cross-country ski uphill in thick cement boots. The salmon had to swim against this steamroller force of water to reach their spawning grounds. The strength necessary to accomplish such a feat was unimaginable. No wonder so many had died in the attempt. Without Moose to assist, Jim had to retrace his steps twice to pull us to the far side individually. Despite the difficulty of crossing, I found the best thrill simply standing in the water, my feet dry in their waders.

We fished for the next several hours. Jim patiently helped set me up, then stood nearby, offering suggestions for where to cast. This was supposed to have been Moose's job. In short order, I hooked a pink salmon, and the fight was on. Fifteen thrilling minutes later, I brought my catch close to the pool's edge, and Jim netted it before getting the fly out of its mouth. I did not want to keep the fish but did want a photograph to remember the moment. Taking my phone, Jim handed me the squirming fish, then stepped back to snap a picture. Unhappy with the arrangement, the fish whipsawed its whole body furiously. Like a true angler, I shrieked and dropped it in the water, but it was too shallow for the exhausted fish to swim away. On the second try, I held it just long enough for a photo to prove I caught an Alaskan salmon.

We stayed in Prince of Wales for three days. Moose was enthralled with the fishing and could not get enough. He wanted to be on the water first thing and stay until late afternoon. This allowed just enough time to get Moose's daily catch to the small processing plant, where it would be frozen for shipping home. Since we only had one car for the four of us, we planned our days around Moose's preferences. Jim attempted to steer Moose to a more leisurely schedule but ultimately accommodated Moose's enthusiasm, knowing he and Deb had an entire week to do as they pleased once we left. So far, everyone seemed to be making extra effort to facilitate Moose's spirited excitement over the bounty of Alaska's salmon season. Like anyone with a singular focus, Moose didn't notice that others' preferences were sacrificed.

A WHALE OF A TALE

After leaving Prince of Wales Island, we took a series of short, thankfully uneventful flights to get to Sitka. For our stay there, I wanted to go on a sea kayak tour that would hopefully allow us to see humpback whales. When I proposed the idea, Moose was equally excited about the chance to get on the water to explore. I had asked him to handle the booking, but he hadn't managed to get around to it. Ultimately, I made the arrangements myself. More and more, I noticed that his inability to follow through was a recurring theme, like an old record that always skips at the same point in the song.

September is outside the main tourist season, but one outfitter was still willing to offer us a guided tour. Not surprisingly, we were the only ones on it. We met our guide, Mitch, a science teacher in his thirties, at the outfitter's shack near the harbor. After signing our waivers and listening to Mitch's talk on safety and basics, Moose and I carried our tandem kayak to the water. I shimmied into the small cockpit in the bow while Moose did likewise in the stern. The snug fit would help with bracing while we paddled. Mitch sat in his kayak offshore, waiting for us. Once he saw that we were set, he turned toward open water. We followed.

We had told Mitch that we were hoping to see whales. He said that was a real possibility if we were willing and able to do several miles of diligent paddling to reach a spot where he had seen whales the previous day. Moose and I both agreed. We paddled away for the first hour, quickly getting into an efficient rhythm to keep up with Mitch's pace. There was no need to talk as there was plenty to see—an endless blue vault arching overhead, forested islands on the horizon in the distance, an emerald-green buoy being used for lounging by a family of sea lions, and something large and winged gliding over the coved shoreline far away.

My ears were covered with a wool cap, but I could still hear our paddles entering and exiting the water and the crunch of the hull slicing through the gentle waves. We crossed the harbor and continued across Sitka Sound toward Cape Burunof. Occasionally, Mitch would turn his head and shout encouragement, but mostly, we focused on covering the necessary distance. My arms and shoulders were tiring when Mitch brought his kayak alongside ours and pointed to a misty column about a football field away. It was a whale spout. Naturally, we wanted a closer view, so we all paddled toward the sighting with renewed vigor. More spouts erupted, meaning that we were among several whales. Mitch told us to aim our kayak ahead of where the whales seemed to be swimming. Hopefully, we would intersect them.

I put my head down, focusing on paddling hard. Then, right as I looked up, a humpback surfaced just fifty feet ahead. It's startling to see an animal that huge, that close, especially when a tiny plastic kayak is the only thing between you and it. Believing we were near enough, I stopped paddling, the natural result of adrenaline-tinged fear. Not Moose. With all his might, he dug in faster to get us even closer. Being in the front of the kayak, I felt particularly vulnerable. Not that it would have mattered if the whale decided to come up under our craft and knock us both into the sea. I turned to look at Moose over my shoulder. "Are you crazy?" I asked. He was.

Smiling as though lit from within, he shook his head in joyful wonder. A few yards away but behind us, Mitch called over to suggest I bang on the side of the kayak so the whale would know where we were. I enthusiastically banged the hull a few times, stowed my paddle, and readied my camera. I definitely wanted a few pictures. Fortunately, the whale had no designs on our lives and could swim faster than Moose could paddle. With a huge splash, the whale breached again, spraying my face as it flipped its tail flukes. I held my breath and snapped a photo before suggesting that we back off.

This wasn't the first time Moose had pursued wildlife in a way that bordered on foolhardiness. Once, we had been biking on a rail trail when a two-foot black snake slithered across our path. We both stopped, but Moose got off his bike, picked up a nearby stick, and quickly chased the snake up the slope bordering the trail. The snake circled some underbrush, made a U-turn, and headed in my direction, Moose in pursuit. I yelled and backed out of the way. The hunter and the hunted crisscrossed the trail a few times before the snake had had enough. It stopped, stood straight up a few feet from Moose, and hissed. I felt the same way.

"Enough!" I admonished him. "Leave it alone."

"Okay, okay," he said. "I just wanted to hold it."

The whale incident added another weight to the negative side of my Moose scale. It indicated a careless disregard for consequences or others' safety when he locked in on pursuing creatures in the wild, whether it was fish, snakes, or even a whale. I realized that something about hunting and catching transported him, so his focus narrowed in on achieving the objective no matter what. His home was a testament to his success, his walls crammed with the taxidermied heads of his trophies, including his biggest and most treasured prize, a bull moose. Moose's brother once remarked dryly, "He loves animals, dead or alive." It was an obsession I tolerated initially but eventually found to be a source of aversion.

THE WAY I SAW IT

The conclusion I drew during our Alaskan trip went beyond incompatibility with Moose or any one particular person. Yes, I liked having someone to do things with, but I wanted to be met halfway. In the case of Moose, the strength and independence he displayed when we first began dating appeared to crumble when he had me to rely upon. He was too content in allowing me to devise the plans, letting me figure out the specifics by myself, bowing out on the driving and navigating since he wasn't good with technology, and even coasting on my credit card, promising to pay me back after the trip. While he complimented me on how I inspired him to be a better person, I didn't feel challenged to grow in any respect around him, except maybe in patience. Breaking up with him was the obvious conclusion.

When Moose and I began dating, I was open to giving him leeway while we got to know each other, especially in the beginning. I am not alone in entering a new relationship, seeing what I want to see, and emphasizing the positive. There is a fresh magic in imagining the possibilities when you meet someone for the first time and seem to click with them. Their quirks are endearing, at least for a while. Eventually, the quirks may not be endearing, but they are tolerable—until they aren't. In hindsight, it's easy to reevaluate poor decision-making regarding the heart. You forget how your emotions of that time, the other pressures of your life, your general longing for things to work out, and platitudes about the power of love funneled you toward choosing to hang in there beyond a relationship's expiration date.

I also had to examine—to overcome—one of my self-limiting defense mechanisms. I had subconsciously concluded that having a man beside me was fundamentally necessary, as if his presence could bar my psyche from remembering its history of drought. In my twenties, I had a recurring dream. I stood looking over a swath of parched, cracked earth, the heart-scape that should have been watered by unconditional parental love but was dry.

When Mark flowed in, he provided a strong devotion that banished the insecurity of possible depletion. His death not only drained the waterway, but it scraped out an even deeper chasm of pain. Without thought, I reverted to my go-to strategy to find another guy to spoon a few bits of comfort into the canyon of my grief.

Yet, as time went on, I made choices that forced me to reexamine a lot of what I believed about my capabilities and needs. With each circle around the sun, I challenged myself to attempt something new and difficult to live out Mark's legacy. What I had learned along the way changed me, though it took me a while to see this in myself.

For many years, I thought I needed a man to validate my worth. I looked to someone else to provide the scaffolding to bolster my confidence and the dam that would cause acceptance to back up behind it. Eventually, little by little, I realized that I had built my own supporting structures and self-worth had to be a do-it-yourself project. My tools were the annual adventures of my custom-made life. I had taken measure of the situation, hammered a framework, sanded rough places, cut what didn't fit, and assembled a way to do life on my own.

Only when I reached the vantage point where I could acknowledge my strength did I notice that the men I'd been involved with generally couldn't maintain equal footing. They enjoyed the benefit of what I brought to the party but acted as long-term guests, unable or unwilling to share co-host duties. It became more work than I cared to do to ensure that a man was happy. After investing years and emotional energy trying to muscle my life into a mold that included a significant other, I finally realized that being alone had its benefits. It took me a decade of grieving, healing, and growing to come to this conclusion.

My grief was manageable, and my life had grown big enough that I no longer required a man to distract me, validate me, or fill the empty places. This mindset shift caused me to quit looking for love and stop thinking I'd ever remarry. Yes, I would still enjoy a man's companionship, but at long last, I concluded that having it was not indispensable to functioning or happiness.

CHAPTER 12

Can I accept my mental and physical limitations with humility rather than as humiliation?

GOING SOLO

An endpoint was on the horizon. Despite any attempt to override its claim on my life's direction, the pull was incessant and irresistible. My littlest had grown into a young man. Once Carson left for college, our five-bedroom house would fold into silence, the constant gatherings of his extensive network of friends a memory on the shelf.

I'd chosen motherhood rather casually at first, never intending to give up my law career. Then, family circumstances arose, which caused me to reconsider. The math wasn't too difficult. Surely, the world didn't care if there was one less real estate lawyer, but to my children, I was irreplaceable. Decision made, I embraced being a stay-at-home mom with a fierce earnestness that surprised me, a Bryn Mawr career woman. Now that was about to change—a transition to be dreaded. The baton would leave my hand while Carson's race began in earnest. It was his time to run, mine to stand and cheer. As he gained speed, our lives would overlap less while the distance between us increased.

TIME'S UP

Carson was eight when his dad got cancer, ten when he died. Carson reacted to his father's death by leaving the room whenever Mark's name was mentioned or getting in fights with his friends when they talked about doing stuff with their fathers. The reason seemed obvious, but I didn't fully understand Caron's thinking until years later when he shared his college application essay. With insight I didn't know he possessed, he explained that as a ten-year-old, pretending he had never had a father was one way he coped with his grief. In the essay, he also described his dad by drawing several parallels between the indestructible Tilley hat Mark had worn daily and Mark himself. Carson used the hat as a metaphor for his father and the kind of man he himself hoped to become.

Personally, I have amnesia about aspects of life in those first few years as a widow. I was too broken to be the sort of heroic mother you read about in books. Regretfully, there was no do-over. All the teaching I hoped to stuff into those eighteen years was done, as if some expert parenting proctor had announced, "Okay, moms, time's up. Put your pencils down."

Freshman drop-off day was a blur of activity. Carson had packed the car the night before so we could be on the road by 8 a.m. for the two-hour drive to the University of Delaware. He was at the wheel as we made our way out of town, past the playground where, in another lifetime, his dad had pushed him on the swings and taught him to dribble a soccer ball.

I don't remember what we talked about that morning. My son was too excited about starting college to listen to anything I might have had to say, and I was too caught up in wondering how his childhood had slipped through my fingers.

The atmosphere was festive as the incoming class converged on the small college town of Newark, Delaware. Bumper-to-bumper traffic greeted us when we turned down Main Street, where the school's blue and yellow colors were on display everywhere. A moving kaleidoscope of smiling students adorned the sidewalks, Blue Hens flags waved from every lamppost, and shopkeepers had their doors propped open, hoping to entice a visit with colorful sandwich boards announcing freshman discounts.

We made our way to Carson's dorm. Someone gifted in systems engineering had set up an efficient process for quickly unloading cars, helping the newcomer obtain the appropriate key, and directing upperclassmen to shuttle that student's gear from curb to room. We were carried along with the momentum and, in short order, found ourselves crowded inside the assigned space. Carson was rooming with Blaise, his best friend since kindergarten, and our families were close. We had even vacationed together through the years. Blaise and his parents arrived around the same time we did. I felt comforted by their presence, the unhappy awkwardness of leaving Carson buffered by doing so in tandem with friends.

The university folk knew this could be a hard day for parents. A midday freshman welcome event was set up to give families a soft deadline to say their goodbyes. When it was time to go, I reached up to give my 6'5" baby one last hug. He grinned. "Don't worry, Mama Bear. I'm going to make you proud." I turned and left the room, determined not to cry because I wanted to do the same for him.

DISTRACT AND DIVERT

Since Carson's junior year of high school, I had thought about how it would feel when he left for college and I returned to an empty house alone. Being proactive seemed best. If I chose an adventure and immediately had somewhere to go myself, that would offer distraction from the inevitable sadness. Simply visiting another place and doing touristy things wouldn't suffice. Recalibrating my mind to adapt to life's next phase would require full absorption in something challenging.

My favorite trips usually involved altitude, whether skiing in the winter or hiking in the summer. A mountain destination was a foregone conclusion. I also wanted to find an organized, turn-key tour that would put me in the company of other people. Years before, I had gone with my brother to the Canadian Rockies with an outfit that used helicopters to access the remote wilderness. We had a marvelous time. In the intervening decade-plus, the lodge owner had built a via ferrata, Italian for "iron way." A via ferrata is a series of iron pins, footholds, rungs, ladders, and cables bolted into cliffs. First used in the Italian Dolomites around 1880, it allowed local mountain guides to help their clients make an ascent. Via ferratas were also used in World War I to move troops around the borders of Austria and Italy. Navigating through a via ferrata is a cross between rock climbing and scrambling over an obstacle course. What could be more perfect?

If I flew to Banff after leaving Carson on campus, I would have two days alone before meeting with the heli-hiking group. It wasn't a surprise that no one in my social circle thought this would be a fun way to vacation. Oblivious to the metaphor of solo travel by a single mom about to become an empty nester, I locked in the trip with a few clicks on my computer.

PEOPLE WHO NEED PEOPLE

Previously, I had flown alone or gotten to a destination alone, but there had always been someone on the other end to meet me. Solo traveling seemed like something for extroverts who were self-sufficient, confident that they'd be able to meet whatever social needs they had through chance encounters along their way.

I had several concerns about my trip. Being completely by myself without anyone to talk to was one of them. Though an introvert, I'm not a hermit. I prefer to be with one or two other people where the conversation goes back and forth. In a group of strangers, the colliding energies of all the various personalities can be overwhelming. While attempting to get a read on each individual, I usually retreat into silent observation mode. This doesn't make for being either memorable or personable. Though I desire to be with people, I know that my presence isn't what would be called magnetic. Being invited to join the sort of short-term groups that form on a trip tour was unlikely. I do better one-on-one. Would I enjoy traveling alone?

After flying to Calgary, I took a ninety-minute shuttle that pulled into Banff around midnight, depositing me and my duffel bag under the hotel's split timber portico. A chorus of frogs sang hello from the banks of the nearby creek while a welcoming committee of moths danced around the lanterns flanking the entryway. No one of my species was in sight. Eventually, a sleepy clerk emerged from a doorway behind the desk, asked for my passport and credit card, and handed over a key. He gave me a map to find the building housing my room. "It's just a five-minute walk," he said. It wasn't the sort of place with bell staff to assist guests. Hoisting my heavy bag, I turned to tackle the last leg of a day that had begun at sunrise on the East Coast and had included a college drop-off, a seven-hour cross-country flight to Western Canada, clearing customs, and a long drive. Exhaustion, physical and emotional, contributed to my confusion as I circled the grounds twice before finding the correct door to a small room whose best attribute was the bed waiting in its middle.

LIFTOFF

On the first day of the heli-hiking tour, a friendly group of about a dozen met in the lobby, where we mingled around coffee and fresh muffins. People smiled at each other, exchanged names, and said where they were from. In short order, we boarded a bus for a three-hour ride to the helipad located in the outpost of Parson in British Columbia. Serendipitously, there was another single woman traveler. She worked for the tour company in charge, Canadian Mountain Holidays (CMH). We chose side-by-side seats, and before long, we were delving into our respective stories like we'd known each other for years. When the bus finally parked in an open field to wait for our helicopter, I had a new friend.

Not long after that, we were transported to the lodge where we'd stay for the next few days. Having rarely ridden in choppers, this maiden ride was a thrill. My face was inches from the plexiglass as I strained to see everything and watched the copter's shadow sprint over pine forests, rocky peaks, and the sparkling Columbia River far below. The pilot banked over a clearing, allowing us views of a large pond near a modern chalet with a sloped flat roof. We touched down on the front lawn a few moments later. Feeling like a celebrity to have arrived by helicopter, I followed the group up the gravel walkway to the main entrance, marveling that I was here. The manager and several mountain guides stood by the oversized wooden door to welcome us. After getting room assignments, we were instructed to gather in the large, second-floor dining hall for lunch and a talk about what to expect over the next several days. I had just enough time to find my room and peek inside. Like the rest of the lodge, it was simple in design but with details reflecting a thoughtfulness toward comfort.

When I climbed the stairway to the dining room, a four-foot-wide oil painting caught my attention. It showed the narrow catwalk at the pinnacle of the via ferrata. Pausing to look caused me to hold my breath and involuntarily raise my fingertips to press into my cheeks. There before me was the 196-foot-long suspension bridge dangling 1,970 feet in the air between the twin peaks of Mt. Nimbus. The bridge is made of wire cables and strategically positioned wooden planks, spaced far enough apart that you have to look down to see where to put your foot next. Of course, looking down would make you realize just how high you were. The layout is clearly designed to strike fear in the heart of the acrophobic.

In deciding to go on this adventure, crossing this bridge was what I intended to do and what I feared I could not. Heights, particularly open heights, unnerve me. The thought of the bridge gave me vertigo. Swallowing my terror, I turned away from the painting while wondering whether the small supply store located in the lodge's basement had any courage for sale.

Moments later, I entered the dining hall where the downhome smell of freshly baked bread offered soothing comfort. CMH guests and mountain guides ate together at long tables lined up so we could view our spectacular mountain setting. My new friend had saved me a seat, and introductions were made around the table. The remote location, relatively few guests, and communal dining for every meal make visitors quickly feel like family.

After lunch, a summary of the day's agenda, and a helicopter safety briefing, we were divided into groups of eight for our first heli-hike exploring the Selkirk Mountain range. We walked out to the helipad and were whisked to a high meadow that reminded me of the opening scene of *The Sound of Music*. Had I been alone, likely I'd have flung my arms wide and twirled. Everyone else seemed equally enthralled by the scenery—if head turning to take in the vista and broad smiles are any indication. For the next several hours, our guide led us through old-growth forests, alongside spring-fed lakes, and across what looked like a river made of enormous granite boulders which had tumbled into the valley as if some giant hand had swept across the top of the nearby arêtes to knock them there. Thanks to a modern flying machine, this vast mountain wilderness had been presented to our select group in bite-sized luxury. We could enjoy dabbling in its beauty, then get ferried by helicopter back to the lodge for a hot shower, delicious food, and a warm bed. I felt grateful, knowing I was extremely privileged to take this trip and step away from the everyday concerns of my life to come here.

DOING BATTLE WITH EARTH, SKY, AND SELF

Not everyone on the tour had decided to do the via ferrata. Those of us who opted in met at the helipad after breakfast, where we were fitted with helmets and climbing harnesses. Two guides would shepherd us through the course. Perhaps they assumed we knew what we were in for. They were wrong, at least for me. Other than facing the catwalk, I had no idea what this day would entail. That was a good thing. I'd slept poorly the previous night. Thoughts of slipping off the bridge and dangling 2,000 feet in the air circled through my brain.

At least two hours of hard vertical climbing up precipitous rugged cliffs several stories high would be necessary before even getting to the bridge. Fortunately, I didn't know that. Sometimes, it's best just to get started and deal with the details as you go along.

From the start, the day was adrenaline-fueled. After getting my gear on and checked, I stood by the helipad, waiting with nervous anticipation for the distinct sound of the rotors. Barely audible at first, it quickly grew to a sustained roar as the helicopter moved into position overhead. While we crouched, the downwash created a small tornado that threatened to blow us over. Expertly, the pilot lowered his craft until the skids touched down a few feet away. Once we were on board and strapped in, a guide gave the flight crew a hand signal. The helicopter lifted straight up, our stomachs feeling the thrill of its quick ascension until we leveled out and accelerated over the mountains toward our waiting adventure.

We were dropped off in an alpine field quilted with rocks and patches of wild grass. Directly in front of us was the bottom edge of a blanket of broken rock fragments, known as scree, which angled upward toward the base of cliffs. Our guides shouldered their backpacks, and we followed them in a line on the narrow, hard-packed path that led through the scree. Upon reaching the base of the cliff wall that rose forty-five feet above us, everyone stopped. This was the start of the via ferrata and the beginning of our climb. For the initial section, a succession of U-shaped steel rebars, each about a foot wide, had been pounded into the cliff. They were placed in a zigzag pattern just far enough apart to ensure that navigating upward would be interesting. A continuous thick wire cable was also affixed to the cliff to the right of the rebar rungs.

Before the first climber had a go, the guides demonstrated the purpose of the cables. They were a safety system that ran alongside the 1.5-mile length of the via ferrata. You clipped yourself to the cable as you navigated the climb. You did this by using the two leashes, each about four feet long, attached to the waist of your climbing harness. We were shown and reminded of the importance of always connecting the carabiner end of both our leashes to the safety cables. The guide explained that steel eye hooks separated the cables into ten-foot segments. When you reached the end of a segment, you unclipped one of your leashes from the old segment and clipped it onto the new one. Then you did the same for the second leash. You never fully unclipped from the old cable segment until one of your two leashes was attached to the next segment. If you fell, it would still hurt. Probably a lot. Even wearing the harness, you couldn't avoid the effects of gravity and slamming into the mountain. But falling ten feet at most was better than falling all the way to the bottom. Assuming you clipped in correctly, at least one leash always kept you from total disaster.

All morning, we carefully hoisted ourselves up the mountain foot by foot. The journey was not merely climbing. Sometimes, we had to sidle along on ledges barely four inches wide with our cheeks up against the rock or wobble across short sections of tightrope cable suspended over some deep ravine. We plastered ourselves against sharp-edged crags and bent around a ninety-degree rock corner while dangling thirty feet in the air. Occasionally, finding the next toehold or handhold required blind groping and prayer. Anyone who wants to practice being in the moment might consider doing a via ferrata.

My adrenal glands worked overtime to produce the hormone responsible for increased heart rate, muscle strength, blood pressure, and metabolism. Nonetheless, I was still the slowest of the group, my terror of heights counterbalancing my desire to see this adventure through. A guide named Bernie hung back to coach me forward when I couldn't find the next hold or began hyperventilating from panic. His calm and steady voice was my beacon, transmitting encouragement and determination when my signals were getting mixed up and lost. Hours later, the other climbers cheered when I finally hauled myself up over the edge of the open, flat ridge that was the designated lunch spot. They had all gotten there ahead of me.

The plan was to take a forty-five-minute break before tackling the final phase of the via ferrata, which included the nightmarish catwalk suspension bridge. We sat on boulders and opened backpacks, grateful for sandwiches and protein bars. Laughter and chit-chat echoed off the cliffs and settled around me. I took a few deep, shaky breaths. Gradually, my heart rate slowed, and I relaxed a bit, relieved to sit on the small plateau above the tree line. Around us were serrated peaks, granite plates shoved skyward, and scraps of snow in the shaded ridges of broken rock. While there was more to come, I could be still and look at the distant mountain peaks, feeling a sense of accomplishment at having gotten this far.

After a time, Bernie approached me and crouched down so we were eye to eye.

"How are you feeling?" he asked.

"Good. Pumped up. Exhilarated and a bit tired," I said.

"Well, I'd like you to consider whether you've had enough."

What? I looked into his face, my furrowed brow letting him know I was unsure what he meant.

"What you've done so far was challenging," he explained, "but the climb is even more difficult after this point. This ledge is the last place we can land a helicopter to take you back down. If you go forward and get into trouble, it will require an aerial rescue, putting you, the pilot, and the team in serious danger." He paused. "I'm not telling you what to do or that you can't try. I am saying, Jennifer, if you decide to continue, there will be much suffering." He stood up. "Let me know what you decide. We're heading out in ten minutes."

Watching Bernie's receding back, my head buzzed, stung by the suggestion that I wasn't up to the task. Pride and a lifetime's worth of messages about the nobility of pushing through pain or fear made me want to prove him wrong. But then, I reflected on his words. "There will be much suffering."

Hadn't there already been enough suffering throughout all those years I had grieved, forcing myself to keep rowing against the stagnating effect of losing my husband so tragically early? Hadn't Mark already been honored through this attempt to live fully, all the way to the edge and beyond the limits of where I felt comfortable? What about the fact that to go on would foolishly put others at risk, all because I was too prideful to admit defeat? Was defeat even an appropriate label for simply acknowledging I had already done enough? I already was enough?

Once again, pencils down. Standing, I squared my shoulders, smiled, and walked to the guide.

"Okay," I said. "You can send the helicopter to pick me up."

He looked at me and nodded. "You made a good choice."

After accepting that I would not finish the via ferrata, I sat and watched the rest of the group head off while awaiting my ride. Being the one left back didn't bolster my self-esteem, but I knew I'd done the right thing. When the chopper arrived, a grinning mountain guide stepped out to help me aboard. To my surprise, instead of going to the lodge, the guide and I were whisked to my private decompression chamber consisting of a quiet, wildflower-encrusted valley with a gurgling stream meandering through the center. The ground beneath my feet was flat and solid. Instead of me being in the sky, it was overhead. The fearful, exhilarated tension I'd been carrying slipped off my back and tiptoed away. Getting across the bridge of terror, something that had seemed important when the day started, no longer mattered.

THE MEANING OF SUCCESS

Have you ever set out to do something for reasons you could only partially articulate, then halfway into it, realize that it's not exactly what you thought? Really, what had you thought anyway? If you aren't sure of your motives or truth, then forks in the road can cause hesitation, confusion, or both.

Socrates is credited with saying that "the unexamined life is not worth living." Yet most of the time, it is only in hindsight and by forcing ourselves to reflect that we can discern what we ought to carry forward from an experience. Sometimes, our first thoughts deserve revision after holding them to the light. When the guide suggested I'd gone far enough, my initial feeling was disappointment. Despite entering the ring to wrestle with my acrophobia, I'd failed to pin it. Physically speaking, I was capable of climbing the cliffs and strolling across the suspension bridge, but doing so when my brain was standing on the brakes in mortal terror was unnecessary. Accepting personal limitations with grace and self-compassion is a different struggle.

A "NO, THANK YOU" SERVING

When my children were small, we served them various foods, not all of which they preferred. The family rule was that when new foods were offered, they could not refuse them entirely but could accept a "no, thank you" portion. This was a smaller taste rather than a full serving. Sometimes, a child discovered that she truly liked this food, but even if she didn't, she was praised for trying it. In the case of me and the via ferrata, I had dished this out to myself, so in some sense, I felt obligated to eat the whole thing. Why had it seemed so important to finish a certain flavor of daring adventure once I realized it no longer appealed and I'd had enough? This wasn't a clean-your-plate situation.

Ultimately, I accepted my limitations because I didn't want to put others at risk. I also knew there was a potential that I'd get seriously hurt. Those on the via ferrata with me had all heard the story of a previous guest, about my age, who had also been warned not to continue but proceeded anyway. She slipped and fell attempting to rappel the backside of the mountain, broke her leg in the process, and had to be rescued by a guide lowered from a helicopter on a hoist cable. That was more adventure than I wanted.

Once the surface waters of my letdown settled, the image reflecting back was satisfying. Though I hadn't done the entire via ferrata, I'd pushed through my fear and completed a significant portion of the course. I had also reined in my pride rather than allowing it to steer my choice. Looking at the situation objectively, I would have said to anyone else that the attempt was sufficient, the decision to stop a good one. Knowing "when to fold 'em" indicates wisdom over foolishness.

For me, I just needed to connect one more dot. The guide's question, "Have you had enough?" had bigger existential implications. Had I had enough of berating myself for how things outside my jurisdiction turned out, enough of thinking that I was inadequate? Had I had enough of walking through the valley of the shadow of death? Finally, after all these years, I could see that the answers were all *yes*.

Maybe it should not have been a surprise that the source of these affirmative responses circled back to Mark. He unintentionally gave me a mission and a gift when he said, "I just don't want to be forgotten." After I stumbled onto the idea of doing legacy challenges to live fully in his honor, I inadvertently found the vehicle that encouraged me to try new things, grow into a bigger person, go places, meet people, and ultimately realize that life could be good again. All those years of naming a challenge and accomplishing what I set out to do created a positive trajectory that strengthened me. Answering the question, "Have you had enough?" helped me realize that it was acceptable to back down. I could try some new adventure and decide on a "no, thank you" portion, satisfied that Mark's memory was kept alive in the mere attempt. I could be okay with moving in the direction I wanted to go, regardless of the outcome.

CHAPTER 13
Can I truly love again?

YOU MAY ALREADY BE A WINNER

I pulled to the curb in front of my home and opened my mailbox. The last bit of daylight allowed me to see a thick manilla pouch nestled among the bills. Grabbing the pile, I climbed back into my car and sorted through the stack, noting with a sinking feeling that the return address on the pouch listed a prominent Philadelphia law firm.

What trouble now?

When I ripped open the padded envelope and tilted it, out slid a paperback book. My first thought was *I didn't order a book.* Then I looked more carefully at what I held and saw the author's name. Well now. It had been thirty-eight years since I last saw him.

I was a law student working at a downtown firm for the summer. He was a young, hotshot associate, the rising star of the litigation department. For nine months, we had dated. In the back of my jewelry box still sat an antique cameo pin he gave me one evening. Ultimately, we went our separate ways after I sensed he was more interested in his career than me.

Then I met Mark. We had different but compatible personalities, bonded over our mutual interest in being outdoors and staying active, and found each other irresistible. Together, we built a home that was our sanctuary and lived quiet lives centered on our family. But after his death, locusts in the form of depression, loneliness, and despair had methodically devoured the once flourishing landscape. With all that had happened, could I even remember being twenty-five and carefree? The young woman I'd once been was just a memory encased in a vague sweetness I could no longer taste.

There was no note to accompany the book, only an impressive business card, his signature, and a cryptic inscription—"Blast from the past. Hope you are well."

The book's arrival was mysterious, exciting, and, frankly, a little creepy. I'd left Philadelphia and had changed names and careers. How much sleuthing had Old Flame done to find me? Still, in a small way, it felt nice that he thought of me after all this time.

That weekend, I read Flame's book and was quickly impressed. He had compiled a series of essays he'd written about his law practice, including a few behind-the-scenes vignettes from representing major rock stars like The Rolling Stones and Madonna. His author's bio indicated that he was a single dad of three. A few days later, I emailed him a simple thank-you, adding a few lines about my family and new nursing career. I mentioned seeing someone so as not to give the wrong impression. That same night, I received a newsy, funny response. Being a writer, Flame expressed himself well, yet he was refreshingly candid that his life was also not perfect.

The surprise of reconnecting with someone whose path intertwined with mine during our twenties before diverging completely for thirty-plus years caused me to wonder what happened to him, his career, and various people we knew from work. What was it like to meet Mick Jagger and be on tour backstage? I couldn't help but email back. Again, he quickly responded. At first, we emailed every few days. These emails were often the only chance to delve into more interesting subjects than the surface chit-chat that constituted most of my interactions with people. He must have found some pleasure in the ongoing dialogue because, as time passed, our emails increased in frequency until they eventually became a consistent, daily thing.

The first phase of this engaging, sometimes lengthy, and increasingly revealing correspondence lasted seven weeks. By email alone, our communication allowed us to share thoughts faster than the typical ways people might get to know one another. We discussed taboo subjects—politics, religion, money—and art, children, relationships, and daily events. I hadn't realized how starved I was for true conversation until I found Flame, or in actuality, until he found me. Each email brought out some new facet of our thinking, made me laugh, or caused me to consider these subjects at more profound levels. Eventually, I asked why he sent his book to me. Flame claimed he sent his first published book to a handful of people who had once meant something to him but with whom he had lost touch. In thinking of his list, I came to mind.

One evening, I showed some of these emails to my girlfriends. They looked at me and raised questioning eyebrows.

"What are you going to do about Mr. Pen Pal?"

"I really don't know."

I didn't want to think too hard about the implications of communicating with a smart, funny, and intriguing man. The girlfriend posse was one step ahead, knowing that because I was involved with Ace again, a choice would need to be made at some point.

Ace returned to the picture after I broke up with Moose. We bumped into one another by accident. Initially, sparks flew, and we seemed to have a new appreciation for each other's positive qualities, but within a few months, we had devolved into our previously existing state of coasting along in neutral. Since my Alaskan trip, however, I had pivoted on the issue of wanting a man to be central to my life, so I was fine with that.

My sister, however, was not. "Don't you want more?" she probed, referring to how my reconnection with Ace had resumed its prior course. To her way of thinking, I was settling.

"No. I'm good," I responded.

And I was. When Ace and I first met, I thought I wanted to find a deep love connection and get remarried, but the years of Ace sidestepping a commitment had worn my heart down. I stopped believing that more was even possible. Eventually, I realized that a man's love wasn't critical, so I embraced the idea that mere companionship was my best choice. When Ace came back into my life, I was fine with his inability to commit because I no longer wanted that from him. Besides, Ace's predictability allowed me to feel in control regarding matters of the heart.

Ace and I seemed to have an unspoken understanding. After all, as sixty-somethings, we appeared satisfied to have a steady, familiar someone to play the role of significant other. He had never really wanted to make the arrangement permanent, and now, seven years of dating later, I could see the benefits of letting that hope go. My freedom from expectations gave me choices and felt empowering. Sure, we could turn up the volume and pay attention. On those occasions when we did, there were mutual feelings akin to love, but mostly our song blended into the background of whatever else was going on in our individual lives.

At the time it happened, I told Ace that an old boyfriend sent me his book. Ace thought nothing of it or at least didn't ask anything about the book or former boyfriend. Thereafter, I kept the ongoing emails with Flame to myself. It didn't seem like anything important at first. *Why create unnecessary turbulence?*

QUESTIONS, QUESTIONS

As my girlfriends and I continued our conversation over glasses of sauvignon blanc, one of them offered a suggestion about my pen-pal.

"You should play the question game," she said.

"What's that?"

We leaned forward as she explained that she and her new husband played this game while dating. She would email him five thought-provoking questions. He would email back his answers; then, she had to respond to the same questions. In the next round, he got to pose questions. They had fun doing this, and some fascinating discussions ensued. She recommended I ask both men the same questions to see what happened.

The next day, I did.

When I laid out the game's parameters to Ace, he thought it was silly but reluctantly agreed to try it. I also emailed Flame, explaining the idea, and sent the same questions to both. Naturally, neither man knew I was also asking the other.

"Describe 1) an appealing scent, 2) a guilty pleasure, 3) a book you recently enjoyed, 4) your preference for a beach, mountain, or city vacation, and 5) an outfit you like to see on the opposite sex."

Ten days later, Ace still had not answered the questions. "I don't know what scent appeals to me," he said.

I offered suggestions. "Freshly baked bread? Christmas evergreens? Newly cut lumber?"

He couldn't decide, didn't see the point, and told me as much. I didn't blame him for being reluctant to try this attempt to unveil and share our thoughts. It can take effort to talk about how you think. That had always been my thing, not his. Introducing this way to reengage after we had dated for so many years probably seemed strange to him, but then he added, "Besides, I already know everything about you."

His remark caused me to lift my chin and look directly into his eyes. He blinked at me from behind his glasses, either not seeing or choosing to ignore the impact of his comment. The clear implication was that there was nothing new to know about me; all had been heard. In short, further discussion of what I thought about anything was not worth the effort and was, therefore, unnecessary. Mutual coasting in a relationship was one thing, but I was trying to get us to be more. He wasn't interested. Any hope I'd had for a deeper connection was flattened beneath his heel.

So, here's where we are, I concluded, my mind picturing those couples who sit across from each other at a restaurant, silent except for the sound of cutlery against plates. The game had been useless, or so I thought.

BACHELOR NUMBER TWO'S RESPONSES

Meanwhile, Flame and I were on question round three by then, each round more specific and intriguing than the last.

1. Superpower you wish you had.
2. Secret crush on a celebrity.
3. Favorite Christmas tradition.
4. A comfort food you enjoy (bonus reveal: who makes it best).
5. What would mean more to you—a thoughtful gift or word?

Thinking of interesting questions or answering his was becoming a preoccupation. Starting the day by picking up where we'd left off in our conversation was something I relished. Yet, because our communication was by email only, it was similar to reading a book. I enjoyed the story and was eager to read more, but it wasn't part of my real, everyday life. I felt far enough removed physically that emailing Flame didn't seem to be a conflicting entanglement, though it certainly had momentum.

By round five, we had mailed each other books reflective of our worldviews; he sent one on history and presidential leadership, while I responded with a volume on theology and philosophy. We discussed how he knew from a young age that he needed to escape the stifling racism of his Southern roots. He was intrigued to probe the determined strength that motivated me to become a registered nurse post-widowhood. Meanwhile, the questions kept going back and forth:

1. Two couple dinner party or large cocktail party?
2. Junk food weakness?
3. Do you save or pitch stuff?
4. Yes or no to making to-do lists?
5. A favorite childhood toy?

By the time we reached round thirteen, Flame and I were trading short emails throughout most days. Despite this, we had never spoken on the phone, nor did I want to. I was happy to have found a virtual male counterpart whose way of thinking easily synchronized with mine. We could exchange written ideas and opinions on almost any topic. He responded thoughtfully but did not intrude on my actual life because he lived an hour away. The physical separation resulting from this arrangement suited me perfectly. Then he posed this question in his next email: *would you go with me to the ballet in Philadelphia?*

What? I felt my stomach tighten. I held my breath and reread the question several times. Shutting my computer, I sat still for a moment, then quickly sent a group text to my girlfriends.

"Consult necessary. Can you meet at Ciro's tonight?"

This was beginning to feel like middle school all over again, but I knew that deciding whether to meet Flame face-to-face required input from women who had my best interest at heart. Did I dare consider what might come of this? Also, what were my obligations to Ace?

As we waited for our drinks and food, I passed my phone to one of my girlfriends so she could read Flame's latest email out loud to the group. I didn't want my tone or inflection to influence the outcome.

"J . . . every time I read the story you wrote about Mark, I tear up.... I have never had such deep exchanges with any other woman. I cherish our correspondence.... I find your reserve charming and your caution understandable . . . and yet . . . I have tickets to the Nutcracker.... I would be honored if you would join me." After she finished reading, there was a rising buoyancy as each voice leaned in, waiting to release its verdict.

"Yes! Meet him!"

"He's the male version of you!"

"You'll always wonder if you don't do this."

"I agree. You should meet him."

The vote was unanimous in favor of going to the ballet.

One final question. "But what about Ace? Do you think I should tell him?" I asked.

"Ace knew from the beginning what you wanted. He's had seven years to commit. He can't have it both ways."

"Do you have a ring on your finger? Are you engaged? Does he talk about it?"

"What do you want to do?"

I looked at my friends as they looked at me. Everyone was smiling. I knew what I wanted, and they had given me their blessing. No one thought telling Ace was a good idea at this point. Meeting Flame could turn out to be nothing at all.

WHEN YOU COME TO A FORK IN THE ROAD, TAKE IT

Flame and I met on the steps of the Philadelphia Academy of Music. As he approached, I held up a small cardboard sign: "Handsome Lawyer #1," referencing the part he played in a bar association video. He was charmed. After the ballet, we sat at an elegant, jazzy bar, talked effortlessly for hours, and met again the next day. When we finally parted after a lengthy lunch, he walked me to my car, leaned in, and gave me a single but memorable kiss. My heart pounded the entire drive home, partly from excitement but mostly from fear.

It had taken years to claw my way to the surface of the grief and paralyzing depression that descended after my husband's death, in the wake of which I was left alone to raise our kids. Though drowning in existential despair, I clung to life primarily because of these three little rafts tethered and bobbing behind me in the storm, each fighting crashing waves of their own. I had worked hard to create a life where I was finally content. I returned to school, changed careers, became a nurse, got all three kids through college, made new friends, and had a steady relationship with Ace. I could foresee that getting involved with Flame had the potential to wreck my carefully constructed, safe little harbor of existence. The feelings provoked by Flame's kiss stoked a fire that might easily get out of control, and I needed control to hold my world together. Upon returning home, I emailed Flame that it was lovely to see him, but we should just remain friends.

Flame graciously accepted being in what he called "the friend zone." He told me he was willing to wait if I would reconsider, but he was low-key about it, a reassuring posture. We decided to continue emailing.

Shortly thereafter, during another girlfriend session, one of them pointed out, "I hope you realize you have the wrong guy in 'the friend zone.'" I pondered this for days, remembering all those lonely years after finding myself unexpectedly single in middle age, the longing I once had that I wouldn't always live alone, and the energy I'd wasted trying to force the issue with Ace.

As a newfound widow, when I first returned to the dating scene, well-meaning folks said that when you stop looking for it, love will find you. *Sure*, I'd thought, somewhat cynically. Now, twelve years down the road, I realized that male companionship on the occasions when I wanted it was good enough. I would be okay even if I never found love again. How ironic that what actually occurred was exactly what many had predicted. Only after I'd given up on love had an old flame literally found me.

My friend was right. After considering our seven-year history and his unwillingness to commit, Ace was the better candidate for the friend zone. Once again, it was time to change gears and move forward. Whatever was going to happen with Flame needed to be explored. I was apprehensive but excited. And hopeful. Flame and I began dating a few weeks later, and once again, we intertwined, this time with a sweetness born of age, prior heartache, and wisdom.

The following spring, we went to Greece together. From the terrace of a cliffside restaurant in Ios, we watched the sun dip below the dancing waves of the Aegean Sea. Moments later, Flame surprised me with a diamond ring. As in a movie, time slowed while I considered his proposal. My first journey across marital love's ocean had brought me so much joy, yet the loss I'd endured had nearly wrecked my soul. Dare I risk another voyage?

Wait . . . dare I not?

I took a breath, slipped my moorings, and then answered yes.

ON BECOMING A POLYGAMIST

One writer likened her post-widowhood second marriage to a form of polygamy. I agree. My first marriage to a beloved spouse did not end voluntarily, and my love for him survives even though he did not. Flame understands this and offers me his full attention when I tell stories about Mark or recall memories of our life together.

"I wish I'd met him," he says, not a trace of jealousy in his tone.

As my friends readily point out, Mark was a tough act to follow. Yet thirteen years passed between Mark's death and getting remarried. Comparison between the two situations is impossible. Mark and I met in our twenties. Beginning with a clean slate, we created a family, home, and business. We were like two pieces of construction paper lined up and glued together—not just at the corners but generously throughout the middle, each year adding more adhesive. When death pulled us apart, the "me" half was a sad mishmash of rips, holes, and torn edges. Over time, I found ways to repair a lot of the damage, but the life I now inhabit is different as a result—and so am I.

Even though I would have preferred to grow old with Mark, when that option was erased, I was left with several complex problems. These emerged as life questions—how to navigate grief, how to ensure that Mark wasn't forgotten, how to be a good-enough single mom, how to find a new purpose, and how to face certain childhood demons. In responding to them, I was forced to cultivate qualities that had lain dormant and possibly would have remained dormant. No one would choose to lose a beloved to an early death, but, like other experiences that seem like pure manure, they can be the fertilizer that brings about unexpected growth. The person I've become, the one Flame fell in love with, is a result of all that.

Now, whenever I glance down, the gold band encircling the third finger of my left hand catches the light. This relatively new ring is stacked on top of the one from my first marriage. I wear the original wedding ring to symbolize that the imprint of Mark's love and the legacy of his life will always be part of who I am.

Flame and I recognize that our ability to love each other has dripped through time's distillery. The product is potent and deserves not to be wasted. Gratitude, grace, and laughter are its complimentary flavors. I can pour this honeyed liquid into the antique glass representing my life and then sip, savor, and truly appreciate how beautifully it sparkles against the light.

EPILOGUE
Can I inspire others with my story?

We often stand a little straighter when someone believes in us, someone who says, "That thing you are doing is good. Keep at it." In my case, first as my love interest and then as my husband, Flame encouraged me to work on my writing. For starters, he suggested I tell the story of why I decided to become a nurse after a career as a lawyer. So, I did. Thinking about what had happened, finding the words to express my family's experience with cancer, death, and grief, explaining how this tragedy motivated me to become a nurse, and trying to tell all of it compellingly were challenges I enjoyed. The essay I wrote was not only accepted for publication by The Philadelphia Lawyer magazine, but they also made it their cover story. The editorial board's affirmative comments on my writing gave me the confidence to continue.

I can't recall when the thought of creating a book popped to the surface. Several of the adventures I'd completed seemed story-worthy, but to what end? What did it matter that an ordinary, middle-aged widow decided to attempt doing annual challenges in her husband's memory? Vaunting about what I'd had the time and resources to do seemed self-aggrandizing unless something in this thinking might light a candle for others. If I stepped back, what had I learned through what I did that was worth being passed on?

Ultimately, I realized how finding meaningful ways to

remember a loved one and honor that person's legacy could help anyone move forward and find a new purpose. Carrying a legacy can be a motivating force for doing intentional acts of generosity, bravery, kindness, or love. This was and is a worthwhile endeavor—one that offers hope for transformation. Writing a book about this idea would allow me to share this message with anyone grieving the loss of a loved one. Readers could consider whether the strategy of taking action to live out some of the positive qualities of their person might be a tool they could use to cope, find new purpose, and honor.

Another motivating force for writing was to demonstrate what healing and resilience might look like. When newly widowed, I wanted to meet another widow who could lead the way and show me that happiness was indeed possible. I never found such a person. One of the goals for this book is to offer others what I longed for—a story of hope.

Though I had no idea how to begin, I decided that book writing could be my legacy challenge for year fifteen. Like all the other challenges before it, this was an opportunity to live fully, requiring effort and perseverance while attempting something novel, big, and scary. Learning what goes into writing a book has required a new skill set and involved meeting people who have left a deep impact. Along the way, writing helped me examine my memories, draw conclusions, and figure out how these events shaped me and our family.

As I wrote, I wondered whether this book would ever make it into print, would ever be read by anyone not related to me, or would possibly make a positive difference in the lives of other people who grieve. One of my main purposes—to honor Mark's memory and show that his life mattered and still matters—would be fulfilled regardless. Often, we must take the first step with whatever courage we can muster, persevere despite whatever seeks to keep us small, and hope that it will all turn out. Unless we attempt to go further than what is comfortable, we don't know what we can achieve.

ACKNOWLEDGMENTS

The life and example of my first husband, Mark H. Hassel, MD, led me to undertake the adventures and challenges described in this book. The story would not have been told, however, without the encouragement of my now husband, M. Kelly Tillery. He nurtured my initial attempts at writing, gave me feedback, and asked insightful questions that pushed me to think on a deeper level. His unwavering belief in me kept me going whenever I got frustrated or overwhelmed. His tears when he read portions of my story affirmed that I'd gotten it down in a meaningful way. I am and will remain grateful for his love and support.

Many others helped me during the years it took to conceive of and then complete *Badass Grief* and also deserve to be thanked. Once I decided to begin dabbling in writing, I stumbled onto an online writing course by author Holley Gerth. Often you don't hear how your work impacts another, but hers was deeply meaningful to me even though we have never met. Holley's online course "Be a Kick-Butt Writer by Friday" got me to the starting line of thinking I might be a writer. She also shared information with her students about a writer's group called Hope*Writers, which, for me, was a game changer. Thank you, Holley.

Thank you also to Dr. Brian Dixon, Emily P. Freeman, and Gary Moreland, who each mentored me during the year-long Hope*Writers 2021 Mastermind. Your combined expertise gave me the tools to hone my writing craft and, equally necessary, understand how writing a manuscript is just one piece of the process of creating a book. Brian, you taught me to consider the reader first and the importance of knowing the who, why, and how of the specific audience I intended to help through my writing. Emily, your insights helped coalesce my story and offered me direction at critical points when I felt lost or uncertain. Gary, I held onto your words of affirmation whenever I doubted myself or wondered whether I had anything worth sharing.

I was fortunate to meet author and memoir editor, Marion Roach Smith, who saw in my rough drafts the fragments of "a hero's journey." Marion helped me rewrite the manuscript to tighten the story and tell it in a compelling way. Her astute perceptions allowed me to connect memories to larger themes. Marion, I'm grateful to you. Your encouragement bolstered my belief in myself and in this project.

Thank you to author Molly Breazeale who read several of my earliest drafts and saw the pattern that ultimately became this book's structure. Thank you to writers Kathy Izard and Meredith Carpenter, and my friend Theresa Stengel, who each read drafts of certain chapters and offered helpful suggestions for improvement.

Thank you to my brother, author David R. Evanson, for devoting hours upon hours to helping me with marketing. Thank you to my sister, Leslie Enos, who is always in my corner. I am grateful to each of you for your love, support, and encouragement.

Thank you to Pastor Steve Cornell for walking beside Mark through all nineteen months of Mark's cancer treatment, driving us to Johns Hopkins every other week for chemo, sitting with Mark through every single all-day session, and being the manifestation of God's very real presence to us when we desperately needed you. Thank you also for sharing your thoughts on the example of Mark's life during his eulogy: live fully, laugh often, serve others, suffer courageously, be faithful, love nature, love God. I have held onto each of these seven statements all these years. The first one was the impetus for what became my annual legacy challenges and ultimately this book.

Thank you to my children, Erin, Emilee, and Carson. My love for you motivated me to get up and press on whenever thoughts of quitting overwhelmed me. Now that you are grown, I watch you embrace adventure and challenge in your own lives. I am proud that each of you is carrying on your dad's legacy in your own way, using your inner strengths and particular gifts. You have taught me, stretched me, and brought me joy. I am grateful for you.

www.ingramcontent.com/pod-product-compliance
Lightning Source LLC
LaVergne TN
LVHW041810060526
838201LV00046B/1195